Captain Alexander Stewart t[...] [...]
Cameronians (Scottish Rifles) in May 1915 and was posted
to France in March 1916. He served at the Somme and at
Passchendaele, and was awarded the Military Cross in July
1917, before being wounded and sent home in October.
On his return he married Margarita MacDonald with whom
he had two sons, William and Thomas. He died in 1965
aged eighty-three.

Cameron Stewart is Captain Alexander Stewart's grandson.
He is an actor who works extensively in UK television,
theatre and radio. His production of *My Grandfather's Great
War*, a one-man show based on the diaries, recieved *The
Stage* nomination for Best Solo Performance at the Edinburgh
Festival in 2008.

CAPTAIN ALEXANDER STEWART

A VERY UNIMPORTANT OFFICER

My grandfather's great war

CAMERON STEWART

HISTORICAL CONSULTANT: JONATHAN BOFF

HODDER

First published in Great Britain in 2008 by Hodder & Stoughton
An Hachette Livre UK company

First published in paperback in 2009

1

A CIP catalogue record for this title is available from the British Library

ISBN 978 0 340 97712 5

Typeset in Bembo by Hewer Text UK Ltd, Edinburgh

Printed and bound by Clays Ltd, St Ives plc

Hodder & Stoughton policy is to use papers that are natural, renewable
and recyclable products and made from wood grown in sustainable
forests. The logging and manufacturing processes are expected to
conform to the environmental regulations of the country of origin.

Hodder & Stoughton Ltd
338 Euston Road
London NW1 3BH

www.hodder.co.uk

To

Thomas Howard Stewart

(Alexander Stewart's son, and my father)

Contents

A Note on the Illustrations

With no mass telephonic communication, and no easy access to photographic equipment, postcards were the picture text messaging of the First World War. Containing only short notes – sometimes only the date – they were the quickest and easiest way to keep others informed of one's continuing existence, and frequently heralded the sending of a longer, more time-consuming letter. Pictures of places on the postcards often gave an indication of one's approximate whereabouts, though security issues decreed that captioned place names were often pencilled or cut out.

My grandfather asked those to whom he sent the postcards to save them so that he could retain a pictorial record of his experiences. He left behind a few photographs and many albums of postcards sent and received both prior to and during the war, so the majority of illustrations in the following pages are taken from this private collection. When messages on the back are thought to be of interest, they are quoted in the captions.

Photographs from public archives are used to supplement these images wherever it has been considered that they might clarify an event or issue of particular importance to the narrative.

Foreword

by Cameron Stewart, grandson of Capt. A. J. H. Stewart

I am four years old and too small to go in the boat, so holding my mother's hand I squelch down across the heather to the lochside in my rubber boots, feeling the wind and the drizzle on my face, hearing the creak of the rowlocks as the dinghy scrapes ashore over the shingle and drinking in the myriad smells – the fish in the bottom of the boat, the heather, Grandpa's damp tweed coat, his pipe. Later, I gaze fascinated as he slurps his soup in the bright hotel dining room.

It seems incredible to me now, but I knew the man who wrote this diary, who lived through what you are about to read, and though I was only about six years old when he died, the memories of that period are vivid. The smell of Angostura bitters – and doubtless gin – in the antique cabinet as he poured the evening drinks in my grandparents' sitting-room in their flat in Eastbourne; the little box room in which I slept, with the wooden chair by the window where I could sit after dark and look down at the lights in the glistening wet street below; talking to my grandmother in the kitchen at the back of the flat with the – I now realise – very 1950s implements and décor; the journeys to Scotland with my mother and grand-father on the night train; above all, the smells (is it my imagination, or did things smell different then?) – the bitters, the wood, the pipe tobacco, greased fishing lines . . . and freshly caught trout.

Approach fifty, and time takes on a new perspective. Today's teenagers may consider the years of their parents' adolescence to be the Dark Ages, but to us they seem bewilderingly immediate, even if the images present them-selves in faded pastels of Kodachrome rather than digital high definition. We realise that to half the guests at our christening, the end of the First World War, the Bolshevik Revolution and the Roaring Twenties were as vivid as the 60s and 70s are to us. Then imagination starts leaping back in 50-year increments and suddenly the Battle of Waterloo is only four middle-aged people away, and the Battle of Hastings only twelve or thirteen elderly people. The continuity of history presents itself with new relevance.

Apart from some unsuccessful attempts by my uncle (himself a founder member of the Special Boat Service in the Second World War) to get this diary published in the 1960s, it has been gathering dust on family bookshelves for nearly eighty years. I remember my mother mentioning its existence to me a number of times, but it did not come into my hands until a visit to my father (who is now eighty-four) earlier this year. So why did it languish for so long? And why the decision to publish it now?

I know my uncle was demoralised by his inability to generate interest in the diary in the 1960s, but I suspect that much of the problem lay in its still being too recent, in the same way that when I was at school in the 1960s and 70s the Second World War – now, I am told, a central element in the history curriculum – was not touched on. 'History' ran backwards from about 1920; anything within the previous forty years wasn't really thought of as history, and we were supposed to know about it by some kind of osmotic process from our parents – the trouble being that they didn't much want to talk about it. Rather than even conceive of 'counselling' to deal with the sorts of trauma they had lived through, both my parents' and grand-parents' generations resorted to keeping quiet. It wouldn't do any good to drag it all up again, and regimental loyalty and reputation were imperatives.

The reasons for publishing now are a mix of the personal and the general. Personal, because I possess it, because I knew the man, because when I look at photographs of him as a younger man I feel some sort of connection – whether that is pure fancy or not – and because my father is still alive, as are a very few of the people who also lived through this horror; the thread is not yet completely broken.

On a more general level, because although these events were not actually all that long ago, my grandfather and these men he fought alongside had a system of values and an approach to life that appears almost totally alien to us now. When I read the entries, I am of course astonished at the bravery, but at the same time dumbfounded at the insanity of it all.

To a generation that grew up in the 60s and 70s for whom war, although not a forgotten phenomenon, has become either a distant horror or something that manifests itself as perpetual low-grade tension punctuated by terrorist outrages, the type of carnage my grandfather lived through is almost incomprehensible. We have of course heard much of this from numerous novelists, but what strikes me most forcibly about this diary is the apparently phlegmatic and even sanguine approach my grandfather – and it would seem the majority of his fellow combatants – took to their predicament. The courage of these men was extraordinary; all the more so because it was, in fact, ordinary. They were giants – I am at once proud to be the descendant of such a man and ashamed when I think of the fuss my peers and I have on occasion made about the comparatively minor trials which have beset us.

So, again, why now? There are three main reasons. First and second, we can learn from both the bad and the good. We need as many reminders as we can get of our latent insanity as a species, to help us guard against this kind of obscenity happening again. As set against this, we would do well to note the values and emulate the fortitude and discipline of these men as we address the more subtle but no less pressing challenges which present themselves in our own time.

And finally, tyranny and evil are still with us, and it is still the ordinary man who bears the brunt of the suffering and oppression. Perhaps we need to do what they did not, perhaps we need to learn to lay down our arms and shout, as Peter Finch's character advocated in the film *Network* sixty years later, 'I'm a human being, goddammit. My life has value. I'm as mad as hell and I'm not going to take this any more!'

Maybe . . . one day.

Cameron Stewart
Bristol
March 2008

INTRODUCTION

The British Army in 1916

The British army that my grandfather joined in France in 1916 was nothing like that which had gone to war two years earlier. The army of 1914 was largely a colonial gendarmerie designed to police the empire. The regular infantry was organised in regiments, such as the Cameronians (Scottish Rifles). Each regiment would have two battalions, one of which would generally serve in Britain or Ireland, while the other was stationed in the colonies. The battalions would rarely expect to serve together, or even to meet. Behind the 250,000-man regular army stood the Territorial Force, part-time soldiers detailed for home defence in the event of war. The City of London Yeomanry, of which my grandfather had been a member, was a Territorial unit. A further source of manpower was the Special Reserve, composed of men who had completed full recruit training for six months and then spent a month each year back with the colours.

The arrival of the BEF at Le Havre, August 1914.

The British Expeditionary Force (BEF) initially crossed to France in August 1914, 100,000 strong and professional regular soldiers to a man. Largely destroyed in the savage fighting of that year, especially at the First Battle of Ypres, it had been remade, and greatly expanded. The gaps left by 1914 were filled in three ways. First, Territorial reservists were mobilised. Secondly, recruits flocked to Kitchener's 'New Armies' and were formed into the famous 'Pals Battalions' of men from the same district or workplace, such as the 'Stockbrokers' Battalion' or the 'Hull Tradesmen'.

Thirdly, men like my grandfather and, most famously, Siegfried Sassoon and Robert Graves, used personal connections, and some level of military experience garnered in the Officer Training Corps at school or university, to obtain commissions into the regular army via the Special Reserve. All, at this stage, were volunteers. The first conscripts would not reach France until the second half of 1916.

By the spring of 1916, the BEF had more than a million men and was still growing. Not every single man was a fighting soldier, of course. To keep such a large force housed, fed, clothed and supplied was in itself a giant task and required hundreds of thousands of support personnel, ranging from lorry drivers to bakers, and from clerks to road-menders. For example, the postal service alone handled some five million letters per week, with an efficiency we can only dream of today. To put this administrative effort in context, there were only eight cities in Europe with a population of more than a million at this time. The British improvised a ninth in the huts and tents of Flanders and northern France.

The BEF was commanded from General Headquarters (GHQ) by General Sir Douglas Haig. Beneath him were four, later five, armies, each of which consisted of about 200,000 men organised into between two and five corps. One corps would command from two to five divisions.

A panoramic view of a BEF camp at Fricourt Valley.

Corps and armies tended to remain in one place, responsible always for much the same sector of the front. Divisions, on the other hand, were the strategic building blocks of the BEF. Their composition rarely changed, and they would be moved from corps to corps as the situation demanded. This is one of the reasons for the repeated moves of which my grandfather complains.

A division, commanded by a major general, was made up of three infantry brigades, each of four battalions, plus artillery and other units. It would number about fifteen thousand men. The battalion was the soldier's immediate home and family. Under a lieutenant colonel, a battalion counted around a thousand men at full strength, divided into four companies: A, B, C and D. Each company would

normally be led by a captain, assisted by lieutenants and second lieutenants, and be further split into four platoons. Not all 1,000 would go into action, however. Often around a hundred would be sick, on leave, away on courses, or detached for other duties. Another 150–200 would be administrative and transport personnel, left at the so-called 'B Echelon'. Finally, about another hundred fighting soldiers would be left behind as a 'Battle Surplus'. Officially, this was designed to leave a core on which the battalion could be reconstituted in the event of particularly heavy battle casualties. Highly qualified personnel, such as instructors and certain specialists, would routinely be held back. Unofficially, this policy also provided a way to rest those who were tired, whose nerves were unravelling, who were thought to deserve a break, or who were, like my grandfather's cook McDougal, just 'unsuited for the more violent forms of warfare'. Thus, a full-strength company going into action might be 120–150 men strong, led by three or four officers; a battalion might total some six hundred. Casualties would obviously reduce this.

My grandfather's unit was the 1st Battalion, the Cameronians (Scottish Rifles). A proud Scots battalion, it claimed descent from the 26th Regiment of Foot, which had fought with Marlborough at Blenheim. In 1916–17, the battalion served in the 19th Brigade as part of the 33rd Division. Alongside it in the brigade were 2nd Royal Welch Fusiliers, 20th Royal Fusiliers and the sister 5/6th Scottish Rifles. Siegfried Sassoon and Robert Graves both served in the 2nd Royal Welch Fusiliers. The two classic war memoirs they produced, *Memoirs of an Infantry Officer* and *Goodbye to All That*, frequently cast a fascinating sidelight on my grandfather's recollections.

By the time my grandfather joined up, the First World War was already nearly a year old. It had confounded predictions by lasting so long. 1st Battalion, the Cameronians crossed to France in August 1914 as part of the original British Expeditionary Force sent to help defend France and Belgium from the Germans. Everyone expected a war of rapid movement, intense but swiftly decisive. Instead, the defensive power of machine guns and artillery soon created a bloody, prolonged stalemate on the Western

Front; to move in the open in daylight was to die. Only by digging could you protect yourself from the weight of modern firepower. Soldiers under fire hurriedly scraped themselves foxholes, which were then linked up, developed and reinforced. By the end of 1914, across France and Belgium from Switzerland to the sea, entrenched armies, millions strong, glared across no man's land at their enemy.

Both sides extended and deepened their defences. They dug 'support' and 'reserve' trenches to the rear. They built strongpoints, known as 'keeps', designed for all-round

A typical trench 'sap-head'.

7

defence. They drove short trenches, 'saps', forward from the front line to observation and listening posts in no man's land. They erected belts of barbed wire, 20–30 yards deep, fixed to iron stakes, in front of their trenches. They excavated 'dugouts' as much as 30 feet below ground to provide accommodation relatively safe from shellfire. In time, these defensive systems might become thousands of yards deep, like the German 'Hindenburg Line', which my grandfather encountered in May 1917.

There was no such thing as a standard trench. Weather, ground, the tactical situation, the nationality of the original builders: all these would affect construction. Where the water table was high, for example, fortifications might have to be built up above ground with sandbags. Where possible, the sides of the trench might be revetted with wood, but this was by no means universal. 'Funk holes' might be scraped out of the walls of the trench to provide a little more shelter from enemy artillery. Weather and enemy action imposed the need for constant maintenance of the ever-eroding defences. Pioneer and Labour Battalions carried out much of this work, but there were never enough to go around. Consequently, soldiers out of the front line, to their disgust, had their rest repeatedly disturbed to provide 'working parties', carrying materials, digging trenches or building roads.

'Revetments', 'saps', 'keeps': the language of the trenches

was medieval. The war was anything but. A relentless cycle of tactical and technical innovation spawned new weapons and methods. These included some my grandfather mentions, such as the Stokes gun, the Mills bomb, and the use of aerial observation to aid indirect artillery fire. None of these, however, nor even poison gas, proved able to give the attacker an edge over defenders who were themselves innovating no less furiously. Every major attempt, by either side, to overcome the defences on the Western Front in 1915 resulted only in more losses. By the end of that year, the French had suffered a million dead or missing, and British (and Empire) casualties were a little over half a million, of whom some two hundred thousand were dead.

After a lengthy period of training and coast defence duty with the 3rd Battalion, my grandfather left for France, the 1st Battalion and this alien world in March 1916.

One of the strengths of his diary is that it reminds us that some aspects of our image of the Western Front are flawed. The picture we have of trench warfare, of heavily laden soldiers climbing 'over the top' at their officers' whistles, to be massacred by machine guns as they plod through the mud of no man's land, is only a part of the whole. Most soldiers participated in major 'pushes' only rarely. My grandfather is in France for four months before he takes part in the Battle of the Somme. The war is more often for him an affair of tedium and routine, a continuous rotation between front-line duty and 'rest' in the rear. As he points out, on a quiet sector it was sometimes more comfortable at the front than behind the lines. In some areas, a tacit understanding between the opposing sides to 'live and let live' reduced aggression to purely ritual levels.

That said, the front line was inevitably more dangerous than the rear, even when action was small-scale. If you stayed in your trench, German artillery and snipers were a near-constant threat. Or enemy engineers might dig a mine under your trench, pack it with explosive and blow you up with it. My grandfather mentions one such, the largest detonated by the Germans during the war, which obliterated a whole company of 2nd Royal Welch Fusiliers. The crater, some sixty yards across, was named 'Red Dragon Crater', in honour of the regimental badge. Edmund Blunden describes his efforts to fortify 'this devilish hole' in *Undertones of War*; as an officer, he earned a reprimand from his general for indulging in manual labour.

Sometimes, you had to get out of your trench. You might, for example, be 'told off' to repair the wire, crawling into the dark in front of your trench, as my grandfather describes. In addition, patrols were often sent into no man's land, or raiding parties to snatch enemy prisoners. Such activities were designed to increase morale, by giving men something active to do, and to gather intelligence. Raids might also be retaliatory. The Royal Welch, for example, carried out a large-scale raid to avenge the 'Red

Dragon' mine. Grandfather's diary entry for 5 July 1916 laconically notes: 'The RWF make a raid v.g.' Captain J. V. Higginson, who took part, was more fulsome, considering it 'a Mark I success'. Forty-three prisoners were taken, and at least fifteen enemy killed, while British casualties were light. In this kind of warfare, old methods sometimes worked at least as well as modern technology. As Robert Graves says in *Goodbye to All That*, 'for the first time since the eighteenth century the regiment had reverted to the pike: instead of rifle and bayonet, some of the raiders had used butchers' knives secured with medical plaster to the ends of broomsticks'. Another way of keeping busy was to snipe at Germans, as my grandfather does. On occasion, this was seen as sport: at least one officer kept a 'game book' logging his 'bag'.

Just as interesting as my grandfather's descriptions of the reality of trench warfare, however, is his record of life out of the line. When given leisure, soldiers invariably find ways to enjoy it. His references to concert parties, gambling and the occasional treat of fresh fruit, a good restaurant meal or a glimpse of a pretty girl's face make this clear. Sport was another frequent pastime. Football, horse racing and, especially, in my grandfather's case, boxing were very popular: the competition he helps organise was won by a fighter called, presumably without customary military irony, 'Hammer' Lane, who later won an army championship.

Every soldier in every age shares one primary concern: not to kill the enemy; not even to avoid being killed; but his own immediate comfort. 'Where's my food? Where's my bed?' My grandfather notes with amusement the grumbling of ration parties, but he is little different: particularly good, and particularly dirty, billets are recorded religiously, even where nothing else happened that day, and he is particularly scrupulous about logging the event whenever he is afforded the luxury of a bath! He has left us a vivid picture of life as a soldier in the trenches.

The following represents a faithful rendition of the text of my grandfather's diary, written while on active service, and his commentary on it, his 'recollection in tranquillity', written eleven years later in 1928. Any editing has been confined to the occasional correction in punctuation (my father claims that his father's secretary must have just typed it wrong!) and, where names of small towns have been misspelt, or have changed, I have used the correct present-day spelling immediately after the town's first mention.

Cameron Stewart
Bristol
February 2008

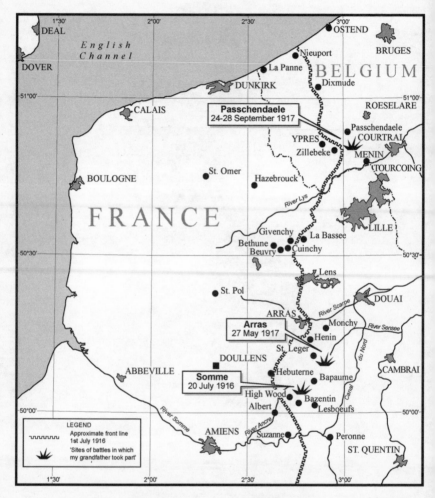

*Map redrawn by Rowland Benbrook from
an original map by Alexander Stewart.*

War

The experiences of a very unimportant
officer in France and Flanders during
1916–1917.

TO MY WIFE

This edition which is in type is limited to three
signed copies of which this is the first.

Alexander Julian Hartley Stewart

PRINCIPALLY for the benefit and perchance instruction of my children in the years to come; partly for the entertainment in the less distant future of my wife and nearest relations; and possibly to a small extent for my own amusement, I propose on the following pages to give a copy of, and comments on, the rough notes made by me in my diary whilst I was in France during the 'Great War' of 1914–1918.

Except for some corrections in the spelling of place names I intend giving an exact copy from the diary without any omissions or additions in the text.

It will be noticed that the notes are extremely brief, and that much that might have been of interest has been rather obviously omitted.

The reason for this is that in the first place, it would have been indiscreet to have given particulars that might have been of use to the enemy, as the writer might at any time have been killed or taken prisoner, and in either case relieved of the diary by German hands. In the second place the notes were all written on active service, often in front-line trenches, where there was not the time or the place or the inclination for lengthy writing.

Unfortunately there seem to have been a good many days on which the diary was left blank. Many no doubt because nothing much of what was then thought to be of interest happened and some because time did not permit.

A week in the front line might easily pass with no event of more interest than a fight between aeroplanes. Aerial combats, although fairly frequent and always very diverting and exciting to watch, would, unless there was something special about them, not be noted. When one's entire sympathies are so very much on one side, to watch, through a strong pair of field glasses, a fight in the air between two or more planes is one of the finest and most exciting sports that can be experienced. In fact we watched with such interest that we did not even make bets on the result. Whilst thinking of the life of our man in the air, we did not forget our own skins down on earth. Our peace and comfort in the trenches very largely depended on the supremacy of our fighting men in the air, and when the Boche came hurling or flopping down to earth cheers went up to heaven from all along our line.

Judging from personal experience it appears obvious that the success of an army in the field primarily depends on the initiative in the air being obtained and maintained.

Nearly every time that an enemy aeroplane was permitted to fly over or behind our outpost line, and to return to its own lines in safety, both our infantry and artillery shortly afterwards suffered from severe and accurate shell fire. I can only recollect one apparent exception to this rule, and this exception may be explained by the Boche observer making a slight error. An enemy plane at dawn flew low over us when we were in a very shallow, roughly-made trench that for certain reasons had been pushed forward about fifteen yards in front of the true front line. In the afternoon we attacked.

In the evening the Boche, expecting a second attack, put down a very heavy and fortunately very accurate barrage from guns of all calibre on the trench fifteen yards behind where we were lying. Our casualties, if any, were negligible.

Any casual comments I may make in these notes will be perfectly candid and in no way expurgated. When reading them it must be borne in mind that a few weeks of war although possibly in many cases improving to a man's character does not lead to great delicacy of feeling. What would seem a devil of a joke in a shell-hole in 'no man's land' might, in the privacy of one's own home, appear somewhat gruesome.

As this is written in the first person it will be difficult to avoid a somewhat frequent use of the word 'I', for which fault I offer my apologies in advance.

My grandfather, Alexander (Tim) Stewart, Malay, 1914.

When the war broke out I was on a rubber estate under contract for four years. I was a private in the Malay States Volunteer Rifles. My agreement expired in, I think, March 1915. I then left Malay for home where I arrived in April 1915. For some weeks I stayed in London and with my brother, Thomas Percy, in Richmond, Surrey. It was in his house that I first met my wife, Rita Macdonald.

For a short time I was laid up with a slight fever and rheumatism. Later I went with my brother for two weeks' fishing holiday at Tomdoun in Scotland; a trip that I look back on with the greatest pleasure. It afforded a fitting and pleasant contrast to my past life in the East as a planter, and to my future life in France as a soldier.

In May or June I went to the War Office with a letter of introduction from my uncle by marriage, Colonel Delavoye, C.B., one time in the 90th Foot 'Scottish Rifles'.

I asked for a commission in my uncle's old regiment The Cameronians (Scottish Rifles).

Shortly afterwards I received an official intimation from the War Office saying that I had been granted a commission in The Cameronians, as an officer in the Special Reserve, and had been posted to the 3rd Battalion. I was instructed to report to a School for Officers in Glasgow on July 1st, 1915.

The reason why I apparently so easily obtained a commission was, apart from my uncle's good offices, probably due to the fact that I could show two years' service in the old volunteers whilst I was at school; one year's service in the then newly originated OTC, also whilst at school; two years' service in the City of London Yeomanry (Sharpshooters) after having left school; and, lastly, four years' service in the Malay States Volunteer Rifles.

On July 1st, 1915, I arrived in Glasgow and reported at the Windsor Hotel together with, I suppose, about fifty others of all classes. In that city I remained for about a month or slightly longer, undergoing a somewhat intensive training, one portion of which consisted of rising early in the morning and running about the streets of Glasgow without hat, coat or waistcoat. The weather was cold, and felt particularly cold to one who had just returned from a very hot climate. The training, although rapid, was good: but Glasgow is not a pleasant city to live in.

When I left Glasgow I was granted a few days' leave and was then ordered to report to my Battalion, the 3rd Scottish Rifles, in Nigg, a place on the east coast of Scotland on the Highland Railway, a bleak and desolate spot which during war time was about thirty hours' journey from London. The camp was about two miles from the railway station, and consisted of a collection of huts made of wooden planks lined in most cases with asbestos sheets. These huts were planted on the moor about one mile from the sea, but separated from it by a range of small hills. The officers' rooms were about fourteen feet by eight.

A small wall stove was provided by a kindly quartermaster department, and needed. The other furniture, which was provided by the occupants, consisted of a canvas camp-bed, a canvas bath and wash-basin and a canvas chair.

Nigg was a very cold place; so were the huts. Camp beds are much warmer to sleep on if paper is laid on them and used as a mattress.

Nigg was not dull – it was nothing. It is not a place; it is a station on the Highland Railway.

Once or twice I got leave and came down to London. When in camp we were kept fairly busy drilling and training. Every night we had to find a guard to watch the coast. The guard of about twenty men and two officers marched off at about sunset to a small fishing village called Balintore, about five miles along the coast, and returned at dawn.

In March 1916 I left Nigg with orders to report for duty in France on a certain date in about a week's time. Not having any great expectations of returning to London at any time I made as good use of my short leave as I could; and so to France and good-bye to home and beauty and all that sort of thing.

The training I received after joining the army and before I was sent overseas was longer than that had by many who were gazetted during the war. It was, I believe, found that any educated man of fair intelligence could easily learn in six months all that was needed. Successfully leading men in war, like most work in life that does not require any special technical knowledge, depends to a great extent on common sense and a shrewd judgement of character, coupled with the capability of subverting fear. I think that all the regular officers, anyhow all those I met up to and including the rank of Major, were splendid fellows; but nevertheless speaking generally I soon came to the very definite opinion that the new 'war officers' were infinitely more capable, led their men better and did their job better than the old pre-war regulars with whom I came into contact. The old regular was frightened of doing anything that was not quite according to Cocker, and to my mind went far too much on the assumption 'theirs not to reason why'; very fine and very brave, but if God has given you a brain why not use it? There were of course very many exceptions but, again speaking generally, it seemed to me that the longer a man had been in the army the less intelligent he was.

One of the many exceptions was my old Colonel, Colonel Chaplin, DSO, etc. He is a splendid example to take because had he not had common sense and moral courage he would have got his Brigade very much sooner than he did. I was told that at Loos he strongly opposed his battalion being sent forward to attack without an artillery barrage. Those over him did not like it, but he was perfectly right as very few, if any, of those who did go 'over the top' ever got to the enemy's front line.

The foregoing has proved somewhat longer than I had

expected would be necessary, so I will pass on to the actual diary without any further preamble or pertinent personal platitudes.

March 21st, 1916. Leave Waterloo for Southampton 12.30 p.m. Boat leaves Southampton 12 midnight. L. & S.W. Rly. S/S Hantonia.

A cold crossing. Boat full of troops. Having taken a bromide I was not sick.

March 22nd. Arrive Havre 12.30 p.m. Leave Havre for Rouen 10 p.m.

Le Havre in the 1900s.

Like most trains in France during the war the train was very full of troops and very slow.

March 23rd. Arrive Rouen 7 a.m. Camp No. 2, I.B.D. 9.30 a.m.

Rouen is about forty-five miles from Le Havre; the train took nine hours. IBD stood, I think, for Infantry Base Depot.

March 24th. It snows.

The camp in Rouen was very similar to the one I had left at Nigg, and was on top of a hill just outside the town.

March 25th. In Rouen.

I do not remember much about Rouen but it was an interesting old-fashioned town, and I believe rather reminded me of Canterbury: with a slow-flowing river, the Seine. There were Red Cross barges on the river, and old castles on the banks.

March 26th. Leave to join 1st Battalion in trenches. Leave Rouen 5.30 p.m.

March 27th. Arrive Béthune at 1 p.m. Arrive trenches 7.30 p.m. Very wet.

483 ROUEN. — *La Cathédrale, vue de face, à l'état actuel.* — LL.

Rouen, *'an interesting, old fashioned town'*.

Rouen to Béthune, 19½ hours in train, distance 120 miles. The reason why the trains always took so long was that very often they would not go direct to their destination. Sometimes, when a passenger, one would go to sleep and wake up to find oneself at most unexpected places. Very often the trains would get on to some siding and stop there for hours on end, and the passengers would get out and wander about the country, generally searching for food or hot drinks. There was always a lot of horn-blowing before the train started.

When I at last arrived in Béthune I went to one of the hotels there and had some food; afterwards reporting to the Captain Quartermaster of the Battalion, who, soon after dusk, handed me over to the quartermaster sergeant and party that was taking rations up to the battalion in the front line. We started off in a horse and trap along the Béthune–La Bassée road. The further we went the worse became the road and the more shell-holes there were on the track and along the sides. In front of us we could see a few shells exploding, guns being fired and Very lights going up. I asked the man who was arriving if the road was often shelled and he replied it was 'sometimes something cruel'. He then I believe did his best, as I was a newcomer, to 'put the wind up me'. As he was a man who lived in Béthune in rest billets and only went up to the trenches with the rations he was only too glad to be able to enlarge upon dangers of his duties, particularly to one who had no experience and was therefore unable to judge or compare. Actually it was far from a pleasant job to have to traverse twice every twenty-four hours in the dark a bad road that was frequently shelled; but infinitely to be preferred to being in a trench for about 100 hours or more at a stretch. Those in the trenches suffered from the same attention from the enemy, and with no place in which to lie down in comfort and rest.

Eventually we got out of the trap and after walking a short distance along the road turned off into a communication trench that started a few yards from the side of the road. Thus I entered the trenches for the first time. The trench was narrow; the men were carrying the rations in sacks (sand bags), it was pitch dark and progress was slow. The trench zigzagged about and there were a few turnings off, but the leader knew the way and on we slowly went, all the time gradually drawing nearer to the exploding shells, sound of rifle fire, and the Very lights. After about an hour we came to a more or less open space where we found men waiting, sent from the companies in the front lines to collect the rations; as usual these men were cursing at the rations being late, but had the rations arrived before them they would have cursed at the rations being too early. This cursing always took place and was a part of trench routine.

The meeting place was by a ruined house, some of the walls of which were still standing: a very bad place to choose, but easy to find in the dark. Soon after we arrived a few small shells came over and landed near us. I was glad to find that the only feeling they aroused in me was one of interest. The men who were with me, and who knew better what these shells could do if they landed nearer, I noticed did not view them with the same equanimity. This also pleased me as being satisfying to my amour-propre, particularly as I thought they looked to see how I was taking it, and made some remark. As soon as these few shells came over several of the men remarked what a blankety blank blanker the Boche was. Many men seemed to get great satisfaction from saying out loud what they privately thought of the Boche.

After a short stay by this ruined house I went with one of the ration parties who took me to the dug-out occupied by Battalion Head Quarters, where I was introduced to Colonel Chaplin who gave me a whiskey and water. In passing, I may mention that although whiskey was one of the most important items of every company mess in the trenches I never on any occasion saw any man the worse for it, and very many times saw men the better for it. After a short talk with the Colonel and others in the dug-out, including the Adjutant, the Doctor, and the Padre, I was sent with a guide to 'C' Company headquarters in another dug-out; here I reported to the O.C. company, a Captain Bannerman I think, and after another drink and some food lay down on the mud floor and so to sleep.

March 28th. In trenches. Very cold.

I believe that the winter of 1916 was the coldest experienced for many years. Except for wet feet and clothes, cold weather in the trenches was not as bad as might be thought, as always being below ground level the full effect of the cold and wind was not experienced to the same extent as above ground.

March 29th. Fire in enemy's trench. Have a shot at a
periscope. Relieved by R.W.F. at 7 p.m. via
Burburie Alley and Lewis Alley.

It was a fairly big fire – most likely a dug-out that had caught alight.

It was a frequent diversion for some of us to creep up just before daybreak and lie down behind the parados (the earth thrown up behind a trench) and then have shots at anything we could see moving in the enemy's lines.

Having been a marksman I rather fancied myself at this sport, and hope I may have bagged a few Boche. There were special men who were good shots told off for this job. It was good sport and the men were very keen on it. Later they were given telescopic sights and armour-piercing bullets to use against steel loopholes. It was not very safe to fire many shots from the same place, and we had several men killed or wounded who were careless in that respect. A very important point was to make no movement.

It was the 2nd Royal Welch Fusiliers who relieved us. The alleys mentioned were the communication trenches that ran back to our reserve line. We had to go by certain alleys so as not to hinder our departure or the incoming troops.

March 30th. Arrive in billets, good, at Bouvrey (*Beuvry*).

Bouvrey was partly inhabited and some of us had beds to sleep on; we also had a mess-room, with a fire, for meals. The men were in empty houses and barns.

In Bouvrey there was an old woman who was reported to be mad. It was said that she had had all her sons killed in the war. Anyhow, in all weather she always sat at her front door, just on the pavement, and held a piece of cardboard to shield her old eyes from the sun, even when no sun shone. All the time she kept looking up and down the road for someone who never came. Every time I went to Bouvrey I saw her.

March 31st. In Bouvrey.

April 1st. Watch anti-aircraft guns in action.

A pretty sight. A bang, a long wait, and then a puff of smoke sometimes near and more often some distance from the plane. Very difficult shooting, as the plane would not go straight but like a snipe zigzag and up and down, so that the gunners had to make a guess as to what direction the plane was going to turn and whether descend or ascend. Not only had the aim to be correct but the fuse to be correctly timed, and this all had to be done at express speed. No wonder so few hits were recorded.

April 2nd. Return to trenches 6 p.m. Two shells burst left of road. In Auchy section. Same dug-out as before.

Three and a half days' rest and then back to trenches. Had I been longer in France I would not have commented on

A wiring party moving up to no man's land.

two shells bursting: however I can remember these two, though I must have forgotten thousands of others. They burst just about thirty yards on our left, in mud, and did no harm. We were on the La Bassée road at the time.

April 3rd. Go out with wiring party on right of twin
  sap. Sniped and bombed. Watch Stokes gun in
  action. Fifty wiz bangs in return.

I had a lot of wiring to do in this part of the line at various times. This was my first night out in 'no man's land', and it is a wonder it was not my last. The men I took out knew it was my first time out and I was afraid of them thinking I was afraid. We made a hell of a noise about it and must have annoyed the Boche, who may have thought we were going to raid them. We drew a lot of rifle fire from their front line, and then they started throwing bombs at us from an old mine crater. This must have awakened a Stokes gun team that had been messing about in our lines. Our Stokes gun then started dropping Stokes bombs into the Boche crater and into their front line; this stopped them sniping and bombing us and enabled us to finish our wiring job which we did well. We then started to return to our dug-out. My dug-out was some way down the communication trench and before I got there the Boche artillery had started to retaliate with a fifteen minute 'hate', no doubt having been urgently requested to do so by their infantry in the

36

front line who were getting our Stokes bombs thrown at them. So ended the little war started by my first wiring party.

April 4th. Go out to lay down barbed wire and lose my way so return home.

It was pitch dark and I had had little experience. Winding zigzag paths were left in our wire to let parties get out into 'no man's land'. Going through our own wire I lost my direction and wandered about for over an hour.

April 5th. Put out wire by German crater. Fletcher, Dillon and Cunningham, damned funny, much sniped at. Good strafe at 11.30 p.m.

Fletcher was a man who always looked scared and had a funny face. What amused me so much was that Fletcher every time we were fired at put his head down, towards the ground, like an ostrich is said to do, and groaned. Dillon and Cunningham were a tough couple.

April 6th. Leave trenches for Bouvrey at 8 p.m.

It will be seen that the so-called 'tour' in the trenches was about four days in and three or four days out. In those days four days under fire was thought to be long enough. Not so later in the war, particularly on the Somme.

April 7th. In billets at Bouvrey.

April 8th. In billets take working party to trenches
   return midnight.

A tedious job going up to the trenches with a working
party. Hard work and not liked by the men who thought
they were being done out of their three days' rest. As a
matter of fact some men preferred being in the trenches
to being in rest, as in many ways they had an easier time
in the trenches, particularly if they didn't have to go on
ration parties.

April 9th. In Bouvrey.

April 10th. Leave Bouvrey for Béthune. In billets at 81
   Rue d'Aire.

April 11th. Hay given out. Raining.

April 12th. In Béthune.

I am not sure that I remember the billets that we were
in, but I think it was here that all we officers of 'C'
Company had our photo taken together; these photographs
I still have. It was not many months before of all those
in the photo I was the only one left.

'France April 1916, C company.'
My grandfather is in the middle of the back row.

It was also I think at this time that one of the men came one day to the mess with about half a dozen fish that he said he had caught; there were no signs of any hook marks. I strongly suspected a Mills bomb. However, we ate the fish and enjoyed them.

April 13th. Go to boxing.

April 14th. Route march. Boxing in afternoon. Theatre at 5.30. Petit Chevaux D'Boy.

The boxing was a Brigade show. I had a good many bets on the various matches, and on balance lost money.

1'r   — Façade du Théâtre. — L.I.

The theatre at Béthune – *'the boxing was here'*.

The show at the theatre was also a Brigade show. One of our men called Daniels (on the Somme I got him the Military Medal) was made up as a girl and was very good in the part. The story went the rounds that some of the young bloods really thought it was a girl and waited for her at the stage door with boxes of chocolates. The story was said to have been true and may well have been so.

April 16th. Play patience.

We played a lot of patience in and out of the trenches. The game was called Gamblers Seven. Generally two people played against each other, each buying and selling the pack for ten francs. A very good game for the trenches as it was short and took up little time or room, and was a good game for a gamble.

April 17th. To theatre in square. 2 p.m.

April 18th. Leave Béthune for trenches at Brickfields. Arrive Brickfields 8 p.m.

This was a rather more interesting part of the line than that we had come from. Where we had been the land was coal-mining ground, with large heaps of old mining spoil, I suppose about fifty to one hundred feet high scattered about the place. In the distance were the so-called towers of Loos.

'The tower was not as here shown last time I saw it.'

The Brickfields was a large area where at one time bricks had been manufactured. There were enormous pyramids of bricks larger than a big house, with the trenches running round them on one side and joining them up. There were also a lot of craters about the place and all the ground was very much mined by us and the Boche. Counter mining was being done all the time. There was one brick stack that, it was rumoured, might go up at any time. It was not healthy on the stack as the Boche sometimes dropped Howitzer shells on top of them. In the trench just behind a stack was the safest place.

Extract from letter dated April 24th:

'On the 18th we left the place where we were resting and returned to another part of the trenches with our left resting on the banks of the canal; our dug-out was under a railway embankment being a sort of culvert and for a dug-out quite large and comfortable. The second night in trenches I had a wiring party out; nobody touched, but our Company Commander who was out digging a new trench was shot through the arm and died. The following night we had a bit of a strafe on, as the Company on our right were out to try and get some German prisoners; there was a short artillery preparation to which the Boche replied. Whilst the strafe was going on all officers had to be with their platoons, to see that all men kept down in their deep dug-outs and to see that the sentries kept their heads over the parapet and a good look-out. Soon after the show started, the Germans started sending wiz bangs over into the front line where I was. I had a lucky escape as at one time I was standing on the fire step with one of the sentries when a shell exploded just the other side of the parados about a yard away from me; fortunately we had heard it coming straight at us and had time to jump down into the trench, where we got covered with dirt, mud and stones, but were unhurt.

'The night after the strafe I was going to go out with a corporal to try to lay out a German patrol; we took six bombs and a revolver and intended to stay out for some time and catch a German patrol unawares; as it was, we spent nearly two hours floundering about amongst our own wire. We had seven to eight aeroplanes in the air; they were flying over the German lines and all the time being fired at; not one of them was hit. I saw about 40 shots fired at one of them before it returned over our line; not a German plane was to be seen.'

April 19th. Wiring party 9 to 10 p.m. Butterfield wounded.

I seemed to go out wiring every night. We were putting out a lot of wire all along this part of the line, as a fair number of raids were taking place.

There was a certain amount of excitement to be gained messing round in 'no man's land' during the night. There were many German dead about and some of our men were very keen on going out gleaning. The important thing to remember was to stay dead still in whatever position one was in if a Very light went up, a very frequent occurrence. We sent up very few, the Boche many, particularly when they were at all 'windy'.

Butterfield who was the O.C. Company was examining our wire when he was wounded; he was shot through the upper part of the leg. He was a nice chap and we were sorry to lose him.

April 20th. In trenches. Strafe at 9.30 p.m. Put two rolls wires out.

April 21st. In trenches, fail to get through our own wire.

It is by no means easy to get through well-laid and deep wire entanglements. Anyhow, I tried for about an hour, without success, and came back feeling a fool.

April 22nd. Leave trenches for Le Quesney (*Le Quesnoy*) at 6 p.m. Sleep in billets.

Cannot quite fix Le Quesney, but fancy it was small dirty mining village.

April 23rd. Take working party to trenches. Brown
  comes as my servant.

Brown was a funny sort of man, a good servant, rather interfering, but always kept my things very well. A man who took the war and me rather seriously. I think he was killed, but forget when.

April 24th. Take party to bathe Anaquin (*Annequin*)
  North.

April 26th. Return to trenches 6.15 p.m.

April 27th. In trenches at Brickfields. Out wiring
  9.30 p.m.

April 29th. Out on patrol 9.15–9.50. Strafe starts 9.30
  p.m.

Thirty-five minutes wandering about in 'no man's land' looking for Boche patrols and trying to examine their wire. There were, I expect, about five of us in the patrol. If the patrol were an important one the men would be carefully selected for their stout hearts, otherwise they would be detailed by the Sergeant Major. We generally went out armed with rifles and fixed bayonets covered in sacking, Mills bombs and revolvers.

April 30th. Leave trenches 8 p.m. for Les Quesnoy.

Cannot remember which place Les Quesnoy was.

Extract from letter dated April 30th:

'Yesterday I heard the sound of machine guns firing up in the air and someone called out that two aeroplanes were having a fight. I had my very powerful field glasses in my hand so at once turned them on to the place where I could see the two aeroplanes. Just as I turned my glasses on to them there was a short burst of fire from the uppermost one and I saw the other turn over to one side and start turning round and round on its way to earth. One side of it seemed to have crumpled up, and this caused it to twist round just like those things that fall off plane trees, and that children like to throw up into the air and watch coming down. The duel had taken place over the German lines. After the aeroplane had been falling for about two seconds (and all the time I had been watching through my glasses) I saw a man fall out and drop straight down into the German lines, whilst the aeroplane continued twisting round and round, slowly drifting down with the wind towards our lines.'

May 1st. In Les Quesnoy in billets, fine day. No. 9 Platoon beats No. 10 at football 3–1.

Whichever place Les Quesnoy was we evidently had a roof over our heads, as the diary mentions 'billets'. My platoon was No. 10.

May 2nd. Go to Anazin (*Annezin*) to sit on Brigade Boxing Committee.

May 3rd. Meeting about boxing 12 noon.

May 4th. Leave Le Quesnoy for Anazin 3 p.m.

May 5th. In Anazin. Billets and kit inspected 10 a.m. Boxing 5 p.m.

May 6th. R.W.F. boxing tournament. Newman beaten in the 4th round.

Newman was a lightweight and the best boxer we had; he was also a Company cook; a tall thin man. He was entered for the open lightweight event and we rather expected him to win and backed him accordingly. The

'May 3rd 1916. Not so cold as she looks I should imagine.'

R.W.F. did well over that fight; Newman was not in good training.

May 7th. Committee meeting in the Globe, Béthune at
    2.30 p.m. Lunch Béthune.

The Globe was a very well-known cafe where one could obtain champagne cocktails at a very high price. They generally made one ill. Everyone who went into Béthune went in to have a drink at the Globe, and the place was generally full. Only officers were allowed.

I most likely had lunch at an hotel called, I think, the Golden something. One could always get a very good meal there. It was run by three or four girls, sisters. Two of them were quite pretty. One married an English officer and another a sergeant. There was one kilted regiment of which they would allow no member to pass their door. They were I think the Cameron Highlanders.

The story was that one night the regiment in question had a dinner there and some of them becoming somewhat merry kicked up rather a row, and in fact created such a disturbance that they literally frightened to death the old lady who was the mother of the girls. It was reported that some members of the regiment who afterwards went there for a meal were attacked and badly hurt by the daughters.

In Béthune there was also a very well-known boot shop where a very smart looking girl served. Crowds of young

'May 16th 1916. Am leaving this place today,
going up the line. Very fine today.'

officers would go there as often as they could to buy boot
laces. I do not think they succeeded in getting anything
else, or so I was informed.

May 10th. Brigade Boxing tournament.

May 11th. Dentist 3 p.m.

May 12th. Uncle's birthday.

May 16th.   Leave Anazin. Go to Annaquin (*Annequin*)
   South 8 p.m.

Annaquin South was a small mining village about a mile behind our front line. It was only occasionally shelled. I never knew it to be badly shelled. All the inhabitants had left except a very few. There was one old woman who I think lived there, who used to sell oranges, but her stand was nearer the front line, by the entrance to a communication trench.

In Annaquin South I slept on a stone floor and remember how much harder it was than a wooden floor to sleep on. Just opposite our billet was a large fosse, a fosse being a large steep mound or hill of spoil from a coalmine; not a ditch, the English meaning of the word. At the base of this fosse on the ground level, we had a gun emplacement dug into the mound, on the opposite side to the front line. Sometimes the gun would be pulled out, pop off a few shells, and then be pushed back.

Very often, the Boche would fire back and generally either hit the top of the mound or go right over. It was all right so long as their aim was accurate, but if their shells landed a little to the right, they were liable to interrupt a football match taking place on the ground between our billet and the fosse. The firing of this gun was not approved of by the infantry.

May 17th. Went up to trenches with working party
8 p.m. return 12 p.m.

We were six days in Annaquin, which was more or less the reserve line for that part of the trenches.

May 22nd. Leave Annaquin for trenches. No. 10
   platoon in Lewis Keep. Murie joins Battalion.

These Keeps were strong points jotted along our line. They consisted of a more or less circular trench interlaced with smaller trenches. The whole 'Keep' would have a diameter of about thirty yards and would be manned by from one platoon to a full Company. The trenches leading into the Keeps sometimes had doors in them made of barbed wire on a framework. As most of the 'Keeps' were four hundred to eight hundred yards behind the front line it was easy and safe work surrounding them with wire entanglements during the night.

May 23rd. Strafe 4 p.m. 10.30 p.m.

May 24th. Strafe 12.15 a.m. 2.30 a.m. Stand to 3 a.m.
   and 10 p.m.

'Stand to' means that every man has to take up his position in the trenches, with rifle loaded and bayonet fixed, officers keeping on the move. 'Stand to' was only ordered at half an hour before day-break, at dusk and at any other time that an attack might be expected. The two days' shelling had, I suppose, made us a bit anxious and led us to expect a Boche attack.

May 26th. Mine goes up 2 p.m.

This mine was put up by the Boche. A lot of the 2nd R.W.F. who were occupying the front line went up with it. They lost nearly the whole of one company. The Boche then sent over a raiding party who were, of course, very much helped by the confusion. They inflicted further casualties, and occupied a part of the front line and penetrated into the support line. We no doubt would have

A Labour Battalion in a quarry at Beaumont Hammel.

been sent up to turn them out but in no circumstances were the garrison of a Keep allowed to leave it.

There was a party of men working in one of the communication trenches. This party comprised a company from a Labour Battalion, all rather old men not meant to take any active part in the fighting.

These Labour Battalions mostly consisted of strong but elderly navvies, armed with rifles that they knew very little about. To keep their rifles clean whilst they were working they kept them wrapped up in flannel, sacking and/or long bags. Each man carried a pick, shovel and a mouthful of profanity. When these men saw and heard the mine go up they started blasting and swearing, and, picking up the implements of their trade, started to clear off home saying it was a ****** war. Their officer when he heard that the Boche was occupying our trenches suggested to some of his old men that were near that they should 'go up to turn the ******s out'. The men thought it quite a good idea and shouted the news down to their mates. The whole mob, and they were nothing but an undisciplined mob, turned round and started off at a slow pace for the front line. When they got near where the front line was they found the trenches all blown up, and, seeing the Boche about the place, those in front broke into a trot and firmly gripping a pick or shovel burst upon the astounded enemy. Using their new weapons of warfare with great skill, vigour and effect they soon cleared out all the Boche except those that had been picked or shovelled. They then hurried home, no doubt feeling rather ashamed at having done work outside their union.

The crater made by this mine was called the Welch Crater.

May 27th. Leave trenches 9 p.m. Stay in Annaquin South.

May 29th. Leave Annaquin for Bouvrey.

June 1st. Go for ride 2.30 p.m.

I could always get a horse from the Transport Officer, a Canadian called McFie. He had one or two good horses that had been 'found'. These horses had to be hidden whenever any General came to inspect the Battalion.

June 2nd. Return to trenches. Am attached to Royal Warwickshire Regiment to instruct in trench duties. Dug-out with Ritchie.

The dug-outs in this part of the line were infested with rats. They would frequently walk over one when asleep. I was much troubled by them coming and licking the brilliantine off my hair; for this reason, I had to give up using grease on my head. I never heard of them biting anyone.

The Warwickshire Battalion to which I was attached was making its first visit to the trenches. They knew very little about trench warfare, and had to be looked after every hour of the day and night. The C.O. made all the men shave, a thing we did not do. Their first night I posted all the sentries and showed all the men where they must 'stand to' before dawn in the event of an attack. All the sentries were told that they must keep a sharp look out all the time during the night that they were on 'sentry go'. This meant that they had to stand on the firing step and keep their heads above the parapet. For some reason they were very averse to doing the latter, and I spent the first few hours after dark impressing on them the importance of keeping a sharp look out. If the Germans knew that some fresh troops were in the front line they often made a raid, and I had no desire for any Boche to visit us without due notice being given. I did not dare to take out a patrol as new troops seeing us in 'no man's land' might have got the 'wind up' and all started firing at us.

The night passed without anything happening and at an hour before dawn, I had them all 'standing to'. As luck would have it, the Boche chose that time to start a fairly heavy shelling of our second support or reserve line. I rather feared an attack and the shelling was quite enough to disconcert men who had just been through their first night in the front line. The shells sounded as if they were only just clearing our parapet and, as a result, nearly every sentry poked his head down well below the parapet where, of course, he could not see a damned thing, and this just when we most wanted a sharp look out kept. When I got on the firing step by a sentry and started chatting to him he felt ashamed and saw he had nothing to fear and stood up as straight as could be, but when I passed on to the next man the one I had left would lose confidence and down would go his head. Poor chaps, they had my sympathy; it was the terror of the unknown.

I cursed their officers: I expect I feared a raid. I could see where the shells were landing and so knew what the others did not know, that the trajectory of the shells must be at least twelve feet above our parapet and that so long as the barrage continued on the same place our front line was perfectly safe. I therefore got up on to the parapet and smoking a pipe walked along the front line, stopping now and again to chaff the men in the trench, all the time keeping one eye on the barrage to see that it did not shift. The effect was remarkable: all the men seemed to want to get on the firing step and put their heads up to see the fun. It was, of course, still quite dark. Being no less vain than others are I am still pleased when I remember a remark I heard one of the men afterwards make. One of their officers asked him how they had liked the shelling and he replied something about not liking it much 'but when some bloke walked along the top it gave us confidence'. I don't think those were the exact words but they were to that effect.

The night's amusement was not quite over with the shelling because taking it for granted that the men would 'stand down' when it was daylight I went back to the support line, and on my return to the front line found most of the men looking over the top in broad daylight. It was a wonder none of them were shot. After the experience of the night, this struck me as damned funny.

June 3rd. Put out wire: am driven in by rifle grenades.

No wonder, considering the noise made by the wiring party on their first visit to 'no man's land'.

June 4th. Big strafe at night. We take one prisoner.

A trench raid; we, I think, had one killed and one or two wounded. The higher command were very anxious to take prisoners in order to find out what German troops were occupying the line in that section.

June 5th. Alston goes on patrol his first time out.

Alston was a young chap of about nineteen who came from Glasgow. In 1918, I saw him in hospital in London; one of his legs was then shorter than the other.

June 6th. Raining.

June 8th. Leave firing line Boyau 8 and 9 for Lewis
Keep. Arrive Keep 1.15 a.m. Am relieved by 6th
Warwicks: their first time in the trenches.

Taking over or leaving trenches was always a troublesome
business, particularly if the relieving troops were inexperi-
enced. In theory the troops to be relieved 'stood to' on the
firing step and the incoming troops filed into the trench;
the outgoing troops were then supposed to stand down and
their places taken by the fresh troops. In practice it was not
done exactly like this, and often could not be, owing to
the narrowness of some of the trenches. Anyhow it was
impossible to prevent a lot of crowding and congestion and
noise. If the Boche chose this time to start shelling the front
line it was Hell. During the summer months there was little
time to conclude the relief which should be completed
during the hours of dark as otherwise the troops might be
observed moving out.

Boyau means communication trench.

June 9th. Leave for Annazin. Arrive at 2 a.m.

June 12th. Start bayonet-fighting course.

June 13th. Wet and cold.

50 BÉTHUNE. — L'Allée des Marronniers. — LL.

*June 11th 1916. I want to buy some tea the same as
you sent me, the tea here is not fit to drink. Could you
arrange to have some sent to me.'*

June 14th. Cold and wet.

June 15th. Wet and cold.

June 17th. Finish bayonet course. Leave Annazin for
Le Quesnoy: arrive 9 p.m.

June 19th. Working party in Old Boots trench 4.30 a.m.

June 20th. Leave for trenches: arrive 11 p.m. Shelled
by 5.9 along the La Bassée canal.

- Si j'étais grand . . . .

*June 20th 1916. Went for a ride this afternoon to a place
called B_____. The other night I dreamt I caught some
enormous fish which I had great difficulty in killing.'*

We made our way along the towing path by half platoons with intervals of about fifty yards. Many of the shells landed in the canal, sending up the water for many feet in the air.

June 21st. Working on Windy defence line.

June 22nd. Big mine goes up at 2 a.m. in our support line, followed by big raid and big strafe.

June 23rd. In trenches Windy Corner. Strafe.

June 24th. Strafe.

June 26th. Leave Windy Corner for Orchard Keep. C.H.Q. at Boyau 49. Rain all night.

June 27th. Rain all morning. See Armstrong. On watch 2–4 a.m.

June 28th. Raining hard.

The Road to the Somme

My grandfather, on horseback, leading a company of the Cameronians.

AS 1915 TURNED into 1916, even before my grandfather crossed over to France and received his induction into the brutal realities of trench warfare, planning was under way for a huge new offensive in France. The failure at Gallipoli to knock Germany's ally, Turkey, out of the war had brought home to most that only by defeating the German army, in the main theatre of war, could they grasp victory. A major British effort on the Western Front would also appease the senior partner in this coalition war, France. Large tracts of the country still lay under German occupation, and the French had, on occasion, cause to doubt British commitment to their liberation. Further, a major Allied assault on the Western Front could be coordinated with summer offensives by both Russia and Italy to maximise the strain on Germany and Austria-Hungary. The shortages of trained manpower and, even more, munitions, which had hindered British efforts in 1915, should, it was felt, be resolved by the summer.

The plan called for the French and British armies to attack, side by side, along the River Somme in Picardy. Before planning could proceed far, however, the Germans seized the initiative with an onslaught on the French forts around Verdun, in February 1916. This developed into an immense and vicious battle of attrition, lasting most of the year and sucking in reserves. French involvement in the Somme attack was consequently scaled back from forty-two to eleven divisions in the first onslaught, alongside fourteen British, along a 25-mile front. A week-long artillery bombardment, the heaviest in the world to date, would destroy the German trenches and cut the barbed wire. The infantry would then advance, capture the enemy positions and open the way for cavalry to charge through into the German rear.

Things did not work out like that. At half past seven on the morning of 1 July 1916, over a hundred thousand British troops launched their attack across the open chalk downlands of the Somme. As they advanced across no man's land, many saw, to their horror, that the wire was intact. There had simply not been enough artillery to accomplish every task it had been set, and many of the shells were in any case defective. Worse, as the barrage lifted from the German trenches, the defenders were able to rush up to their still-intact trenches from shelters deep underground and open deadly fire on the exposed British infantry. The result was a bloodbath. Sixty thousand British soldiers became casualties by dusk, one third of them dead. In places, the attackers barely made it out of their own trenches before being cut down. The first day of the Somme has become one of the iconic events of the First World War, a byword for futility and waste.

To abandon the offensive was, however, unthinkable. First, anything that could be done to relieve the pressure on the French at Verdun must be attempted. Secondly, contrary to myth, there had been some important successes to be exploited. Both the French, and those British corps on the right, had made significant progress and captured much of the first line of German defence. The British generals therefore launched a series of attacks to build on these gains. Between 2 and 13 July they launched nearly fifty piecemeal attacks, capturing 20 square miles of ground (compared with three on 1 July), albeit at the cost of another 25,000 casualties. Some of the fiercest fighting was at Mametz Wood, which the 38th (Welsh) Division finally captured on 13 July, at the seventh attempt, having lost 4,000 men. This is the wood, described by Sassoon as 'a desolation of skeleton trees and blackening bodies', in which my grandfather bivouacked on 15 July. He mentions seeing only German dead, like the 'bloated and stinking corpse of a German', noticed by Robert Graves, 'with his back propped against a tree. He had a green face, spectacles, close-shaven hair; black blood was dripping from the nose and beard'. There were British dead, too:

Graves describes a German and a Welshman, lying locked in a fatal embrace. Each had bayoneted the other to death simultaneously.

On 14 July, a bold dawn attack successfully captured the German second line. A wood on the crest of the Longueval ridge, known to the British as High Wood, 1,200 yards away up a gentle slope, now blocked further progress. British infantry, supported by an Indian cavalry brigade, armed with lances, staging one of history's last charges, briefly took it on 14 July, but were unable to hold it for long: as my grandfather describes, his battalion was forced to evacuate the wood on 16 July.

Four days later, his brigade attacked High Wood again. My grandfather describes this very confused action as clearly as anyone can. The German shellfire that hit them as they marched up to their assembly position at the windmill was the same barrage which hit Robert Graves. J. C. Dunn, his Medical Officer, considered it 'a bad chest wound of the kind that few recover from', and Graves was, in fact, reported dead. The attack gained most of its objectives, but casualties were too heavy for the ground won to be held in the face of German shellfire and counter-attacking infantry. 1st Cameronians lost 384 men on 20 July, including over a hundred dead, and were pulled out of the line to rest and refit. The first phase of the Battle of the Somme, for my grandfather, was over.

Diary

THE END of June 1916 saw the end, as far as I was concerned, of more or less peaceful trench warfare. During the period of little more than three months I had been with the battalion we had not had many casualties in 'C' company, I suppose on the average not more than one or two during each visit to the trenches. Many of the men had been with the Battalion in 1914, and nearly all were seasoned troops.

July 1st saw the beginning of the Somme offensive. Although we were not on the Somme on the first of the month it was not long before we were sent down to join in that intensive, prolonged and bitter dog-fight. The most offensive feature of the Somme fighting to my mind was the lice and the stench from the dead bodies. The gas was unpleasant, and the chloride of lime in the water far from nice. One evidently becomes more quickly accustomed to what is seen than to what is smelt, and felt, and no one likes to be an unwilling host.

The chief characteristic of the fighting on the Somme

was the very heavy casualties that the British and the French armies suffered. To my mind every man in the ranks who slowly climbed out of the protecting trench and at the bidding of his officer laboriously started on his journey across 'no man's land' to attack an entrenched enemy deserved the highest honour his country could give him. There was no sound of drum, pipes, or trumpet to encourage him, no gallant charge, no cheers from onlookers, no excitement, only a tired and often very weary man, heavily loaded with ammunition, bombs, kit, gas mask and rifle, getting out with difficulty from his trench where he felt comparatively safe and slowly moving across an open space, with the certain knowledge that it was fairly long odds that he would be killed or wounded. Millions did it and many lived to do it more than once.

These cold-blooded attacks were, I believe, not nearly such a strain on the morale of the officer, they certainly were not to me, and this notwithstanding the fact that it was much longer odds on the officer being killed or wounded. The officer was strengthened by the knowledge that he was directing and leading; that the men were looking to see how he comported himself and that if he showed fear all would see. However, once started the men needed no leading and as the officers were generally killed seldom got it for long.

The rate of progress between the two lines of trenches was about two miles per hour; that is about two minutes to cover 120 yards or less. Two minutes is a long time when every second men round you are being hit. The distance to be covered might be from 50 to 250 yards. In the winter when the mud was deep and thick it might take quite ten minutes to cover a hundred yards, and every step forward was an effort.

The finest thing that ever happened in the trenches was the rum ration, and never was it more needed than on the Somme; and yet some blasted ignorant fool of a General, damned in this world and the next, wanted to stop it, and I believe for a time did. The man must have been worse than the lowest type of criminal, can have had no knowledge of the conditions in which the troops existed, and have been entirely out of touch with the men who were unfortunate enough to have him as their commander. He should have been taken up to the line and frozen in the mud as many men were. I would then very willingly have sat on his head, as he was a danger to the whole army. Curse him. Those who have not spent a night standing, sitting or lying in mud with an east wind blowing and the temperature below freezing point may consider that I am extravagant in my abuse of the men who denied the soldier his rum ration. Those who have will know that I have been too temperate in my language.

The fortitude of the armies on the Somme was wonderful. For many days on end the Battalions engaged would have no rest, and were constantly under heavy shellfire.

For days on end the officers would get what almost amounted to no sleep. This deprivation of sleep particularly applied to Company Commanders who at all hours of the day and night were receiving and sending out orders and casualty returns, etc. Nearly all the hours of dark had to be spent visiting posts and positions.

During the summer of 1916 the flies were an absolute plague, great big fat, sodden, overfed, bloated brutes, blue-bottles and large houseflies. They settled on one's face and food. I have seen them on the roof of a dug-out like a swarm of bees. Most of them must have come from and lived on dead bodies.

My diary from the end of July onwards rather suffered from stress and other occupations. Such as it was, I will now continue to copy and annotate.

July 1st. Three mines go up. Gas sent over on our
   right. Two raids come off.

A busy day and night accompanied by a lot of shelling. The battle of the Somme had started.

July 2nd. Leave Orchard Keep. Go to Givenchy Keep.
   No. 10 and 12 Platoon hold the Keep.

I was put in command at Givenchy Keep with instructions to hold my position in all circumstances and at all costs.

That if the Boche came over we were to 'stick it out', to continue firing at the enemy so long as we could and no surrender. As before explained these Keeps were circular. The idea was that if the enemy broke through our front line trenches he would not be able to continue far without first subduing the various strongholds, scattered along behind the front lines, of which Givenchy Keep was one.

July 3rd. Fine weather. In Givenchy Keep.

July 5th. In same place. The R.W.F. make a raid v.g.
   Many shells in Keep.

That night the Keep was well plastered with shells, but I do not remember anyone being hit. Leaving a few sentries on duty the rest of us retired into dug-outs, an officer occasionally going the rounds to make sure that all was well and a sharp look out kept.

Dug-outs were lighted with candles. Every time a shell exploded in the vicinity the candle flame flickered, and every time a shell exploded near all the blessed candles went out and had to be relighted, resulting in a great waste of matches, much annoyance, and arousing the expectation that the next shell might come into the dug-out and put all our lives out.

July 6th. Leave Givenchy Keep. Arrive Le Prail 7 p.m.
    In billets by canal. Raining. Stay night at Le Prail.

This summer of 1916 appears to have been a very wet
one, so far. Rain did not bother me much. I wore a steel
helmet, heavy long waterproof and trench boots through
none of which could water penetrate. When the so-called
tin helmets were first issued none of us liked them. After
a time I liked mine so much that, when in the trenches,
I never took it off for days on end and always slept in it.
It saved my head from many a nasty bump when going
in and out of dug-outs, quite apart from a feeling of
security they seemed to engender. They saved many lives.

July 7th. In Le Prail. Leave 10 p.m. for Obligan
    (*Oblinghem*).

Many of these places mentioned we only stayed at for a
few hours and I do not remember what they were like.
There was always a lot to do, and when not otherwise
occupied we took what sleep we could get.

July 8th. Arrive Obligan at 3 a.m. Sleep at farm. Leave
    Obligan at 11 a.m. for Forperquet (*Fouquereuil*) Station.
    Breakfast near Station. Entrain at 2.30 p.m. destination
    unknown. Pass through St. Poll (*St Pol-sur-Ternoise*),
    Doullens. Arrive Poulliville (*Poulainville*) 2 a.m. of 9th.

A somewhat tedious journey of twelve hours in a stuffy, very crowded train with little food available, and no lights after dark. A lot of the time was passed arguing about to where we were being taken. At that time we cannot have known anything about the show on the Somme. For all we knew we might have been on our way to Italy.

July 9th. In Poulliville find billet for Mess and self in farm. Share bed with Ritchie. Inspect feet of platoon.

Arriving at 2 a.m. in the pitch dark we found that no arrangements had been made about billets and we had to wander about the village to find accommodation, thus disturbing all the inhabitants who, I think, had not had a British Regiment descend on them before.

July 10th. In same place.

July 11th. At 6 a.m. leave Pouliville and arrive at Daours 9 a.m. Lunch at estaminet on banks of Somme. Bath in meadows bank of Somme. Leave pack.

This was the beginning of our march up to the Somme battle line. Every mile we went we saw more signs of intense activity and more and more troops making their steady progress to the furnace. At Daours they told us that thousands of British troops had been pouring through since the first of the month. My bath consisted of a tub that I filled with water from the river; I remember it was very cold and that some French people annoyed me by watching; however, I enjoyed my bath as it was the first I had had for about three weeks. We slept on the tiled floor of an estaminet on the river. The 'old lady' of the house was annoyed at us being there and abused us.

Here we left our packs and only retained a change of socks, toothbrush and shaving kit, handkerchiefs, etc., which we carried in our haversacks.

July 12th. Leave Daours 2 p.m.. for Buire sur L'Ancre. Arrive 8 p.m. Stay night.

A rather long march, along a dusty road with much traffic on it. The men were in full marching order but without packs. A battalion in marching order covers about 2½ miles per hour, halting at five minutes to the hour for five minutes' rest. We were all in bad training as we had done little marching for many months. The Battalion was, however, in great form as we had heard about our attack on the Somme and seeing all the other troops marching to the battle we thought that we had broken right through the German lines, had won a great victory and that the end of the war was very near. Nor were our spirits damped by the constant stream of motor ambulances that met us on the road. Even the wounded were full of buck and saying that 'things were going fine but casualties rather heavy'; they were, very.

July 13th. Night in Buire. Stand by 2.30 a.m.

As a matter of fact we were up most of the night. The 'night' mentioned was that of the 12th–13th. In the morning, bayonets were sharpened to the accompaniment of many bloody jokes and valorous sentiments.

July 14th. Stand by 10 a.m. Leave Buire 11 a.m. Stop at Bacorde (*Bécordel-Bécourt*). Bivouac 8 p.m. Shelled long range.

This shelling was rather comic; it annoyed everyone so and started the whole battalion cursing. We had been marching all the day and at about 8 p.m. turned off the road to a very big field on our right. Here we piled arms, took off all equipment, and most of the men their jackets as it was a hot night. The field cookers came up and at about dusk we all had a good feed and then prepared to settle down for the night. The post, which seemed to always reach us wherever we were, had arrived; incidentally bringing a new pair of boots for me. All were well fed, happy and contented; reading letters from home by the light of many hastily improvised wood fires. Then, no doubt attracted by the fires, the shelling started, and the order came to take cover in the ditch surrounding the field.

Result pandemonium. I was in the middle of trying on my new boots and changing my socks. My new boots I nearly lost, and when the shelling ceased it was pitch dark and everyone was wandering about trying to find things they had lost. However, there was no more shelling and what was left of the night we spent in sleep to awake at dawn feeling devilish cold. I do not think many were hurt by the shelling, some were I know because I remember hearing the cry I was so often to hear during the ensuing months: 'Stretcher-bearers – stretcher-bearers. Where the hell are those bloody stretcher-bearers?'

July 15th. Rise 2.30 a.m., march to Mametz Wood, arrive 6.30 a.m., lie down. Many tear shells, sleep in open, shelled.

Mametz Wood had only been finally captured a day or two before and was full of German dead. Some had evidently been dead for a long time and the stink in places was appalling. We lay in the open, about fifty yards from the edge of the wood in shell-holes. The German dead on the ground we occupied had been collected and dumped together in old trenches; many I suppose had been covered with earth. There were I believe a few live Boche still to

A gas alarm used to warn of an impending attack.

be found in the wood. All the time occasional odd shells were coming over and we had some men wounded but not many as we were well scattered and the shelling was not heavy, although irksome. All that day we lay in the same place and that night. Tear shells came over and caused us much annoyance; they made the eyes run with tears and irritated the throat and nose. I went to sleep in my gas helmet (we did not have masks in those days) and woke up nearly suffocated. The gas from the tear shells tainted the food, and what with the smell of dead Germans and tear gas my nostrils were much offended.

It was this day that I saw two sights of the war that greatly impressed me. The diagram below will show the position we were in. The ground sloped down from the Wood to the stream shown in blue; the other side of the stream was a rough shell pitted road. On the other side of the road, which ran along the valley, the ground rose steeply to Mametz village.

Facing the road, we saw right away to our right a battery of eighteen-pounders coming along at the trot with mounted officers and N.C.O.s in front and alongside; when they were opposite us they broke into a canter, the

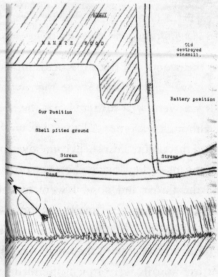

Not to scale and positions only approximate.

guns swaying about as they went over shell-holes and the gunners clinging on like grim death. They quickened their pace and swung round to their left when they came to the road leading up towards the wood. The officer leading then yelled out 'right wheel' and leaving the road, still at a sharp canter, they went on to the open ground. On another order each team of horses wheeled right and halted, another officer galloped to the flank and dressed the guns so that they were perfectly level and facing the enemy; the horses were then unhitched and taken away and immediately all the guns opened fire. The whole movement was done in a surprisingly short time and with the greatest precision although several shells exploded near them during the operation. As the shelling was only intermittent, nearly all the orders could be clearly heard by all the troops on each side of the valley.

The other occurrence that is impressed on my memory was nothing unusual but particularly noticeable because it could be observed by so many. In the valley where two or three tracks met, about four or five officers and men were standing, looking at a map and chatting and smoking. A big shell came over, landed about twenty yards from the group, buried itself in the ground and exploded. Many could hear the shell coming over and looked to see where it would land. When it exploded so near this small group of men, we expected to see some if not all of them laid out. Not one of them was hurt, and the only notice they took of it was that one of the officers strolled over and looked into the hole it had made in the ground.

At this time and place there was comparatively little shelling going on, seldom more than one shell at a time and only every two or three minutes, but what shells did come over were not small ones. One I saw landed just by a man, and lifted him about ten feet off the ground. He went up as if he was being tossed from a blanket with legs and arms moving. He was still alive when he returned to earth.

In this same place just by Mametz Wood one of our officers, a man called Mac something, with whom I was walking, was wounded in the face by a splinter from a big shell we saw explode the other side of the valley – at least four hundred yards away. Which goes to prove that in soft ground a shell exploding near is not so likely to damage one as a shell exploding further away, but to be wounded by one more than four hundred yards off was, I should say, very unusual. In soft and muddy ground, I have several times had shells explode within ten or twenty yards of me, and the only effect they had was to add to my covering of mud. The above remarks do not apply to those shells that were used later in the war and which exploded the instant they touched anything, even a twig or water.

July 16th. Leave Mametz Wood for High Wood 2.30
     a.m. Shelled all the way up there. Sergeant Wall
     wounded, also Findley. Arrive High Wood 3.30 a.m.

Heavy shelling. Christy killed. Watson wounded and many others. Leave Wood 4 p.m. Retire back 1,000 yards to trenches, half dug. Have to leave these trenches at 11.30 p.m. Go to shell-pitted field south of Byzantine le Petite (*Bazentin-le-Petit*). Stay night in shell-hole, raining 12 midnight. Place shelled – move to funk hole.

It will be seen that we only lay for twenty-four hours outside Mametz Wood. It seemed longer and we were not sorry to leave. As it turned out, we went out of the frying pan into the fire. However, the place stank, there was no cover whatsoever, and it is tedious to stay in one open space being shelled and doing nothing. This was my first visit to High Wood, the French name for which was I think Bois Fourneau, Furnace Wood, an apt name as many lives were consumed in it. It was, I say, my first visit, and there can have been very few who returned to it as often as I did. Every time my company went near it, we had many casualties. Sergeant Wall, the same sergeant that I previously mentioned, was my platoon sergeant, and a great help and stand-by in any nasty corner. He was I think wounded on the way up. I forget who Findley was and why I specially mention him as having been wounded. It took us an hour to get to the Wood, but some of the way we were able to go along rough broken-down trenches, but as the Boche were shelling the trenches with heavy guns they did not help us much except to find our way. When we got to the wood, my Company was ordered to occupy the edge on our side, with our left flank on our extreme left of the Wood.

My Company ('C' Company) was the left flank of the Battalion. I was in command of No. 10 platoon. The four platoons of 'C' Company were in the following order facing the enemy and with No. 12 platoon on the left: 12. 11. 10. 9. Christy who was in command of No. 12 led his platoon along the edge of the wood from the right, intending to stop when he came to the left corner end. This he did but probably in the dark went a little past the corner; anyhow him and the first dozen or so of his men who were closely following him were met by a burst of machine gun fire and he and others with him were killed. With the constant shelling, machine gun fire, darkness, and unknown country there was some confusion. We eventually found that the machine gun that had given us so much trouble could enfilade about twenty yards of the left of our position, so we left that part unoccupied. When day broke, we were able to see where we were, attend to our wounded and get the dead out of the way. Christy's body we could not see and anyone who ventured towards that corner of the wood, where we expected he and others must have been lying, was fired at. We could see no signs of any enemy in the wood, which was fairly bare on account of the heavy shelling it had suffered. Soon after daybreak the shelling more or less ceased, but by then our casualties had mounted up and Watson who was in command of No. 11 platoon had rather a bad hole in one of his legs; an artery was severed and he bled a lot.

One of the men in my platoon had had a part of his head removed by a shell splinter. When I first saw him he was lying down, with a lot of grey matter protruding from the opening in his scalp. I thought him dead but as I looked he moved, and moaned, so we pushed back the grey matter and put on a big bandage. Next time I saw him he had pulled the bandages off and was working his arms about. As I thought he was as good as dead I told the stretcher-bearers to get others not so badly wounded away first and this they did. The poor chap with the head wound I just covered over with a ground sheet and left. In my ignorance I did not think he could live long with such a wound; he was of course unconscious.

A few days later, I heard that he had been taken back to the first-aid post and was then still alive. To this day, I upbraid myself for not having given him greater attention.

That morning I climbed one of the trees but could see no signs of any Boche and drew no fire. In the afternoon, one of the men told me that two Germans could be seen collecting wood in front of our little trench. Standing up I could see them very plainly only about forty yards away. I whispered for a rifle; the shot was an absolute sitter and I could not miss. When however I pulled the trigger nothing happened. I swore, the Boche heard, and disappeared. I had not pushed over the safety catch!!

Owing to the enfilade fire from our left a stop had been made in our trench about twenty-five yards from the left edge of the wood; just the other side of this stop a German officer was sitting: he looked asleep but was dead; so far as could be seen he had no wound. One of our stretcher-bearers who was a great collector of souvenirs climbed over the stop and collected his helmet and no doubt went through his pockets. This same stretcher-bearer had found a jar full of rum and having become somewhat tight on the contents was wandering about all over the place regardless of whether he was shot at or not.

That afternoon we discovered that we were very much 'in the air' and that the troops on our left were about 1,500 yards behind us. It was for that reason that at 4 p.m. we retired to some half-dug trenches 1,000 yards to our rear. In these trenches (so-called), we stayed for a few hours but in the middle of the night, we got orders to again move to the rear. We went back to a field that at some time had been heavily shelled, as it was all shell-holes, and we had not been there long before the place was again heavily shelled and once more we had to shift our somewhat tired bodies to other holes in the ground. By this time, it was raining hard, and holes in the ground did not offer ideal sleeping accommodation. However, we knew of none better. A wet hole is better than a dry surface when shells are coming over.

July 17th. Move to Sunken road 2 p.m.

This Sunken road was at right angles to the front line. On the right side, the bank was higher and all along the bank, little caves had been scooped out so that the troops could get some cover. We all wedged ourselves into these holes – one, two, or three in each, head in and feet out. It had stopped raining and the place was not so bad, as everyone's head and most of the body were under cover. I found some coal dust bricks left behind by the Boche and we made a fire and some hot tea and warmed and dried ourselves. The Boche was sending a few shells into the field we had left but none on to the road. The sun came out, we drank, ate and slept and thought what a splendid war it was. Then the Boche spoilt it all by shelling the road with shrapnel; burst, burst, burst all along the road, and one man after another was hit in the leg. They were so tightly packed that they could not pull their legs in under cover. I do not think anyone much minded as the wounded congratulated themselves on getting 'blighty ones': that is, a wound that would send them home but not kill or disfigure. One man however must have allowed the shelling to get on his nerves. The poor chap seemed to go quite mad; he was unwounded but came out of his hole, where he was safe, and ran up the road gibbering and shaking just like a monkey. I went after him but could do nothing with him. He was very troublesome and putting the wind up the others; I am sure he meant no harm and did not know what he was doing. I forget what we did with him at the time and the episode may have taken place the next day, but I remember that the poor fellow became a dangerous pest and that in the end when we moved from the Sunken road I had to order a man to fix his bayonet and to put two inches into the poor mad man if he gave any more trouble. What happened in the end I do not know, but this action had the desired effect and the man gave me no more trouble. Prolonged shelling even without casualties may disturb the brain of the best of us.

July 18th. Raining hard. Funk hole full of water. Still being shelled hard. Conway hit. Oppy and Rusby come to Company. Oppy hit. Rusby down with pneumonia. Move to new spot. At 4 p.m. move again.

Conway was one of the Company officers. Oppy and Rusby, the two new officers, did not last out the day. The reason we kept on moving from one place to another was to try to escape the persistent and accurate shelling that we were experiencing. What a hope!

It was this day I think that I saw some very fine shooting on the part of the Boche. On the top of a cliff about thirty or fifty feet high we had three biggish howitzer guns.

The cliff was roughly parallel to the front line, and the howitzers were on the edge. These guns were firing when a Boche aeroplane came over flying low. Shortly afterwards we heard a big shell coming over and saw it land bang on the left howitzer; it was followed by two others that with the same precision knocked out the other two howitzers. Considering that these howitzers were on the edge of the cliff end and therefore to hit them the Boche had to get almost exact elevation, their shooting was good. The cliff was about fifty yards from where we were lying.

July 19th. Laing joins Company. Fairly fine day. In trenches east of Mametz Wood. At night make advance for attack.

For about four days we had been on the move every few hours and all the time under shell and/or machine gun fire. It seemed longer. We had lost a good many officers and men. We had got rather wet and very muddy. The mail and rations still arrived every day. Five of 'C' Company's officers had been killed or wounded. We generally took four or five officers into action. This day we had still four including myself.

It was always of great interest to me to see the way my fellow officers and friends comported themselves in various circumstances. God knows I had plenty of opportunity of seeing a good many. Some expressed fear but did not show it; some professed no fear and showed none. Some had great fear but showed it to few if any; some were bucked and some depressed. A few showed bravado and generally were afraid. Some became merry and bright and some depressed. Some, a few, showed nothing. I can remember quite a few officers and men who confided to me their fear; to these whenever possible I gave a drink. A drink seemed to give courage to most men – 'in vino veritas est' – and if a man is going to be killed why not be killed when in a cheerful mood? Hence my previous outburst against the **** who stopped the rum issue; may they know fear on a cold morning at day-break. I only knew one man who showed his fear to all, and his brother had just been killed. However, this is a diary and not a physiological (*sic*) study.

July 20th. Attack on Wood [i.e. High Wood] begins at
   3.25 a.m. Attack is held up on the left by rifle and
   machine gun fire. At 3.45 a.m. I drop into shell-hole
   and dig in. At 6 p.m. leave shell-hole for wood,
   attend to wounded, 9 p.m. heavily shelled.

The above gives a very poor idea of what took place. This attack was made with wonderful precision, and was a splendid example of parade ground drill under heavy shell and machine gun fire, and in pitch darkness, coupled with a long march over very broken ground, during which march in open order direction was only maintained by the use of prismatic compasses. I will endeavour to give a detailed description of how the attack was planned and made. It was all done with most commendable precision. The Colonel was told that the Wood, which up to then had been attacked several times by others without success, must be attacked, captured, and retained. These orders he would receive from Brigade Head Quarters. He decided how this should be done, and how and in what formation the Battalion should march to the attack. He knew that about a mile of very broken and heavy ground had to be traversed before we should arrive at the Wood and that all that ground would be subjected to shell fire by the enemy and a part of it to machine gun fire. He knew that the Wood would be subjected to a very severe bombardment by us during the preceding day and during most of the night; that about an hour before the attack an intensive barrage would be put on the whole wood and particularly on the edge; and that this barrage would lift at exactly 3.25 a.m. which would be zero time. He therefore called together the four Company commanders, told them that the wood would receive such a bombardment that nothing could live in it; that the barrage would lift at 3.25 a.m., and that the whole Battalion must then charge, clear the wood and take up a position on the other edge. All very straight-forward and simple.

I may be wrong in small details but in substance the plan for the advance was as follows. Companies were to parade and march off in column of rout at specified times, with intervals of thirty yards between platoons with connecting links; no lights must be shown and no smoking. They were to march along certain tracks to a heap of bricks that had once been a windmill; there each man was to be given extra ammunition and bombs. The Battalion would then continue to advance in column of rout until the order was passed for each company to form a line of platoons in fours with intervals of twenty-five yards between companies and platoons; the formation would then be as follows. This formation was to prevent heavy casualties if we were shelled. It was fortunate.

The Battalion would then continue to advance until 'B' Company was about forty yards from their objective, the right of the Wood. All other platoons would then form

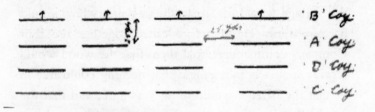

Diagram 1.

two deep, wheel round to their left, and come up in that formation to the left of the Company that had been in front of them. The intervals between Companies and platoons were to be decreased, and position would then be as follows:

Alternate platoons were then to advance about twenty yards and lie down in extended order, the other platoons to remain two deep. Position would then be:

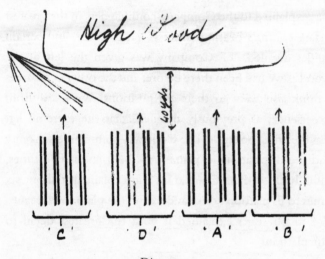

Diagram 2.

Immediately the barrage lifted the extended platoons were to charge, whilst the platoons in two deep were to advance in support and to be used as was found necessary. All this

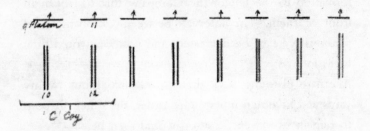

Diagram 3.

was explained to the Company commanders in the greatest detail; compass bearings were given to them, and certain guides detailed. 'C' Company was given the left of the wood as we had been there before, and the other companies I think also went to their old positions. We knew from experience, as previously detailed, that the extreme left was the worst position. The Company commanders, having had the dispositions explained to them about five times, came back to their Companies and explained it about six times to us platoon commanders and the platoon sergeants. We in our turn explained it with the greatest detail to our platoons.

Ritchie was in command of the Company; Laing in command of No. 11 platoon, and McKillop No. 12 platoon. I was in command of my own platoon No. 10, and No. 9.

We started off about 1.30 a.m.; it was pitch dark; I was

with the last platoon. No sooner had we started than the Boche started shelling with heavy stuff the track just in front of us. Ritchie halted the Company and we all got as close to a bank on our right as we could, cursing like Hell at such a bad beginning; however, we had plenty of time, and Ritchie walked back and asked me what I thought about it. I replied that it was a ✶✶✶ but that we had better go on and chance it, keeping a good distance between platoons; he thought the same, so back he goes and leads the leading platoon straight on into the shelling. By the Grace of God just at that moment the Boche altered his range and started shelling behind us and on our right and we got through I believe without anyone being hurt.

We then got on well but slowly, and much to our relief found the heap of bricks that had been a windmill, and the rest of the Battalion before us. It was still very dark but we could see the stars. After a short wait free from shelling we started to advance in the formation as shown in Diagram 1. On account of an unexpected deep new trench and a lot of wire we were held up and messed up and rather lost the formation, but after some further delay we again got into perfect formation as planned. The deep trench and the wire caused a lot of cursing and back-chat, as the troops occupying the trench had evidently taken a lot of trouble in making it and putting out the wire: and we tumbled all over the former and cut the latter to get through. Getting entangled in barbed wire in the dark is no joke.

Well, we continued to slowly advance as if on the parade ground over a flat open space. Then the Boche started shelling again, small shells but plenty of them. I do not think they knew we were there, but were just shelling haphazard. We had a few killed and wounded.

My Company was the last, consequently we passed over the killed and wounded, some of whom we could just recognise. One of the platoon sergeants came to me and said his nerves had gone and a lot more. The poor chap seemed very upset so I gave him a drink from my flask. In a minute or so he was as right as rain and full of gratitude.

Then a man came running up to say that Ritchie had been killed and would I come and look at him to make sure he was dead. Ritchie and I were very friendly. Off I go and find him on his back and so far as I could see quite dead; it was very dark so I could not see him very well. On we go and the shelling still continues.

As casualties occurred the men closed up to keep the formation. I moved from platoon to platoon talking and wanting to smoke. And then who should I run into but Ritchie, who said he had gone up in front to 'D' Company. I was astounded and told him I thought he was dead; he said not yet (he was killed within sixty minutes) and that he had not been touched. So it was some other officer lying dead who I had mistaken in the dark for Ritchie. Largely auto-suggestion, I suppose.

We continued – and so did the shelling. Our pace was, I should say, about 1½ miles per hour. As previously mentioned it was pitch dark and the ground very broken by part-dug trenches, dead, shell-holes, and wounded. I had appointed two 'runners' to take messages who had to follow me close wherever I went. One was a tall thin man, very fair, with a girl's voice; he was a female imper-sonator, and in concert parties behind the line always took the part of a very pretty girl. The reader may think this a curious choice for a position of some importance, as my life might depend on the actions of my runners, especially if we got into a tight corner. But this man, Daniels, although rather nervous and highly-strung, was nevertheless a very brave fellow, and above the usual intelligence; also he liked talking and was never afraid to point out things he thought should be pointed out. Also he had a nervous quizzical way with him that always amused me.

My other 'runner' was a very nice little chap called Daly. A short, small, sturdy man of about thirty. He had been a Company runner for a long time. He never showed any concern whatever was happening. Several times I had seen him jog along with a message through a barrage and arrive smiling all over his face. He was rather deaf, and seldom spoke, and when given a message to take over ground that was being heavily shelled he only grinned. I don't think he ever thought much, but he was a very 'stout' fellow and could be absolutely relied upon to stick to me like a leech. Both these two 'runners' received the M.M. for the night's work and deserved it.

We continued on our way and after a short time got out of the zone that was being shelled; the shelling although persistent and annoying had only been small stuff and our formation had not been broken. After a time owing to the darkness and the slow pace the Battalion got rather bunched up; then by bad luck we got to a patch where the Boche was putting over heavy Crumps – big shells that made a hell of a row and would lay out a whole platoon if they landed in the middle of one. As a result a certain amount of men were hit, platoons got out of order and we began to lose direction. The C.O. halted the leading Company; the men were told to kneel down; the other Companies then regained their proper position and did likewise. The three rear Companies then came up on the left of the leading Company as shown in Diagram 2. In this formation it was more difficult to keep position; however the shelling eased off and we got on quite well. After a time word was passed along to halt and take up the dressing from the centre company and this was done as per drill book. Company commanders then carried on and got their companies into the formation as shown in Diagram 3 above. This movement was done in splendid style and with the greatest precision and exactitude.

Although it was still quite dark and we could not see the wood the barrage by this time had come down on it and we could see where it was. The edge seemed to be one mass of bursting shells that nothing could live in. We had no need to look at our watches to see when zero time came as we knew that as soon as the barrage lifted we had to charge. My position was at the head of No. 10 Platoon and just behind No. 9. I knew we had about five minutes to wait before zero hour and walked along to my right and talked with Laing and then went on in front of No. 10 Platoon and spoke to Ritchie, confirming with him that it was just on time. I then returned to my place at the head of No. 9 Platoon. Ritchie was going to lead in the two front platoons, but must have been killed just after I left him.

Almost as soon as I was back in my place the barrage started to lift and go forward. This is the time the front platoons should have gone forward followed by the two rear platoons. Unfortunately they got no order and did not move. The noise was still so great that one could not make oneself heard, and it was still fairly dark.

I wasted a few precious minutes waiting, doing nothing, wondering why the leading platoons did not advance; and then, realising that something had gone wrong, I ran forward to lead the men into the Wood. As previously explained the two leading platoons of 'C' Company were lying flat on the ground to avoid being hit by any flying splinters from our barrage; now when once troops are lying down in cover it is not an easy matter in the dark to get them all on their feet quickly, very particularly so when the noise is so great that only those near can hear the order, and consequently one cannot reach them all with one's eye or voice. I found that the three or four men near me immediately got up but those on my left and right neither heard nor saw; it was useless to advance with only four or five so I went down the line to get the others up. But we had missed our chance, and every few seconds more and more rifles started firing at us from the edge of the wood and a machine gun started popping off from our left outside the wood; probably the same machine gun that had killed Christy and others on the 16th. Some of the men I got up were hit, then the dawn began to break and we could see the Boche lining the edge of the wood just a few yards in front of us, and blazing away as fast as they could; they were under cover and we when standing up were fully exposed. Nearly all of the last batch of men I got up were knocked out and I realised it was hopeless to try and advance against that fire in daylight. Some of our men were lying down and returning the fire but we were at a great disadvantage as the Boche was in a trench and we were on the level ground. Having no desire to pose as a target I dropped into a small shell-hole and using a big bladed knife started to dig myself in with my hands. The firing for a short time was very intense, but gradually died down. I fear that most of the men who I had been trying to get a move on were killed except those who when they lay down found themselves in a shell-hole. Owing to the fact that I was on the move all the time and kept on the move until I found a good hole to get into, and got into it, the Boche failed to hit me.

There were a certain number of men in shell-holes round about me and judging from what they said most of the Company appeared to have been wiped out. Some of the shell-holes they linked up; most of them were behind me so came under fire from the machine gun on the left.

Every time a man put his head or helmet up it drew fire; some of the men kept putting their helmets up without their head inside; this had the same effect. Not having a rifle I could not fire. I therefore did the next best thing, made myself comfortable and had a drink and pipe, wrote up my diary and dozed. I could hear the men talking in the other shell-holes but they kept fairly quiet for fear of getting bombs heaved at them. In this condition we lay most of that day.

Late in the afternoon I heard a commotion and then saw a company of some English regiment advancing from our right, making an attack on the machine gun that had been giving us so much trouble. They were coming on in splendid style, using the tactics so often practised in peace time and behind the line. Advancing by platoon rushes, officers leading revolvers in hand, whistle to mouth. A blast on the whistle and signal to advance and up got the platoon and doubled about twenty yards; another blast and down they went and another platoon advanced in like manner. It was a pretty and fine sight to watch. The men were well trained. Just as they passed me they came under fire and started suffering casualties; on they went but making shorter rushes. The officer leading was hit.

What happened to them all in the end I know not. All killed or wounded I expect. In actual trench warfare over exposed ground even a Battalion could hardly capture a machine gun in that manner by a direct frontal attack. Anyhow, they showed me that if I ran I could safely get into the wood which evidently no longer was held by the Boche. So off I went very glad to stretch my legs. As soon as I left the shell-hole I started coming upon our killed and wounded. Outside the Wood they were mostly dead. In the Wood were many wounded. I wandered on into the Wood talking to those I met. From the information I gleaned I gathered that on the right we had had no difficulty in entering the Wood and had met with little opposition. The few Boche that had been met with had been killed. The Companies on the right had then strolled on until they got near the outer edge which they found occupied by the enemy; they eventually cleared them out and occupied a shallow trench dug along the edge. The Boche then made a counter attack that was repelled.

In the wood in a large shell-hole I found several of our wounded who could not move themselves. One poor chap had been shot through the stomach and was in very great pain. I told him to wait a minute and I would fix him so that his pain would cease. Getting out my little phial of morphia pills I gave him one and told him to let it dissolve on his tongue. Never have I seen such a wonderful change in a man. He had been groaning and twitching. In a very short time a look of peace came over his face and he said all the pain had gone. I felt I had done the kindest deed of my life and he blessed me.

I then made my way back to our side of the wood with the idea of getting some of our wounded removed. Near the edge I came across the C.O. and one or more officers having a quiet cup of tea and reading the mail! The ration party as usual had come well up to the scratch and through the barrage. Having delivered a dixie of tea and the letters they had returned to the transport line with their tale of our misfortunes and their figurative tail well up at having found us and finished their little job.

Having had a cup of tea and something to eat, I started off to collect what was left of 'C' Company; and damn few could I find – and no officers, as all of them had been killed. Those men I did find, together with some from other companies, I stationed in the trench on the edge of the wood at our side. By this time it was getting dark and the Boche started shelling again. Fearing a strong counter attack the C.O. ordered the trench we were in to be manned and held, and as other men drifted back they were concentrated in this trench. The whole position was very obscure and no one seemed to know what was going on in the Wood and particularly on the other side to us. Those who came from there said that position was very exposed and that very few men were there, certainly not enough to hold that position. Eventually I believe they all came back to where we were. It became quite dark and so far as I know what was left of the battalion was concentrated along the trench on our side of the Wood.

With the darkness the shelling became more intense; most of the shells were bursting in the wood just in front of our trench. Many shells were landing about three to six feet in front of us and covering us with debris. One shell landed just in front of me and so assailed my eardrums that for some minutes I was completely deaf.

Every moment we were expecting a counter attack; and for companionship and to attempt to escape the shelling which was worse on the left, the men started crowding up to the right causing that part of the trench to become very congested. On account of the noise, darkness and confusion it was impossible to guess the extent of our casualties. The trench was very narrow and so shallow that we had to crouch down to escape being hit by shell splinters and earth.

I well remember that I sat on a dead man and smoked a pipe. There was nothing else to do, as it was too dark to see anything even if one risked one's head above the trench; and unless we shouted at the top of our voices we could not make ourselves heard.

(Curiously enough after having added the last two pages I found that I had been writing them without knowing that it was exactly to the hour eleven years after the events chronicled had taken place.)

July 21st. Leave High Wood 2 a.m. Arrive Mametz Wood 3.30. Sleep. Leave Mametz Wood 5.30 p.m. Arrive Buire 10 p.m. Ritchie, Laing, McKillop killed in 'C' Company.

About 1.30 a.m. word was shouted down the trench to prepare to leave as we were going to be relieved. At 2 a.m., as the sole surviving Company officer, I took all that I could collect of the Battalion out of action. All the communication trenches had been and were being shelled to Hell, and on our way back we thought ourselves out of the wood but were worse off. However, after having made a partly voluntary and partly involuntary detour I eventually arrived with about two hundred men at Mametz Wood and there found some of our transport men with some jars of rum.

I immediately dished out a rum ration, going round

The rum ration – here being issued to the Black Watch, July 1916.

with it myself; occasionally standing myself a nip when it was suggested (quite frequently). Then when everyone had had their tot I took one myself, retired into a convenient shell-hole, and so to sleep. The blasted blackguards that tried to stop the soldiers' rum ration should have been taken to High Wood and chained up there for a week. I believe that some of the clergy at home said that the rum ration was teaching the young soldier to drink and for that reason should be stopped. The absence of rum certainly taught the young soldier to swear.

Ritchie, Laing and McKillop (i.e. all the other officers of 'C' Company) were killed, and all the officers of the other Companies except I think one officer whose name I have forgotten.

Back to the Somme

Bazentin Ridge: exhausted soldiers rest after the battle.

IT IS NOT only the first day's butcher's bill that makes the battle of the Somme highly controversial even today. Historians continue to re-fight almost every aspect of it, and if it is ink, rather than blood, which is now spilled, the violence sometimes seems otherwise scarcely reduced. Why did the British keep bashing away at such high cost? Not until the weather broke, in November, did Haig finally call a halt to the offensive. If he was aiming for a breakthrough, he had patently failed. The German line had been pushed back, but was intact. If, on the other hand, as Haig himself later argued, he was seeking to wear out the German army by attrition, it is less clear that the battle was a failure. British losses were enormous: some 432,000 British casualties, including about 100,000 dead. The French had around 90,000 killed. We will never know how many Germans were killed or wounded. Estimates range from 230,000 to over 600,000. Undoubtedly, however, the Germans were shocked by both the resilience and the material superiority of the Allies.

General Pinney.

Throughout the late summer and autumn of 1916, the British launched attack after attack, slowly grinding their way forward in the face of strong resistance. My grandfather's unit found itself back in the line in August, supporting another unsuccessful attack on High Wood. In six days in

the trenches they were subject to heavy shelling and lost
another 152 men, of whom ten were killed outright. The
whole division by now needed a prolonged rest, and so
was transferred for September to a quiet sector away from
the Somme.

While they were there, a new general came to take
over command of 33rd Division: R. J. Pinney. Caricatured
by Sassoon as 'Major-General Whincop', he was a non-
smoking teetotaller notorious for banning the rum ration.
Indeed, he would not even allow his men a tot to celebrate
the Armistice in 1918. Sassoon claims Pinney opposed
the introduction of steel helmets in 1916, on the grounds
that they would make his men soft. My grandfather
describes Pinney as 'always very keen on making attacks,
a damn sight too keen in fact. The troops always said that
he had a glass of blood and cream before breakfast!' Sassoon
took his revenge. Pinney is thought to be the model for
'The General':

'Good-morning; good-morning!' the General said
When we met him last week on our way to the Line,
Now the soldiers he smiled at are most of 'em dead,
And we're cursing his staff for incompetent swine.
'He's a cheery old card', grunted Harry to Jack
As they slogged up to Arras with rifle and pack.

★ ★ ★

But he did for them both by his plan of attack.

A TANK IN ACTION
Canadian Official

Meanwhile, on the Somme on 15 September, the British army used tanks for the first time as part of a large-scale, and mainly successful, assault. Among the positions finally taken was High Wood, for two months now the scene of fierce fighting. How many men died, fighting for those 70 acres, is unknown. It was impossible properly to clear it after the war, and the wood is thought still to contain the remains of some eight thousand men, British and German.

In early October, my grandfather, back in the main battle, is concerned about a proposed attack on Rossignol Wood and takes some leave in case he cannot later. While he is wooing my grandmother with frequent trips to the theatre, the attack is fortunately cancelled. By the last week in October, however, his unit is back in the fighting, and he with it, involved in a series of local attacks towards the village of Le Transloy as the British try to get good jumping-off positions for a major attack to be launched, together with the French, in early November.

Conditions were, if anything, even worse than my grandfather describes. Doctor J. C. Dunn, an experienced old soldier, commented: 'anything I have seen out here yet was picnicking compared with these four days [in the trenches opposite Le Transloy] . . . I shivered in two suits of summer and one suit of winter underclothing; and three pairs of socks in easy boots did not save me from chilblains that made the wearing of boots impossible for two days'. There was little shelter and less firewood against the cold. Troops burnt the crosses from makeshift graves to make tea. Heavy rain had turned the ground to mud reportedly worse even than that at Passchendaele the following year. On 29 October, nonetheless, the battalion attacked Boritska Trench. None got closer than 50 yards to it, and losses were 129 men, of whom 60 were killed or missing.

The last attack of the Battle of the Somme was launched on 13 November. By then it was clear that the weather was too poor to allow further operations, and both armies settled into winter routine. For my grandfather's battalion, that included a St Andrew's Day football match. Their sister 2nd Battalion came to 1st Battalion's 'home' ground and beat them 5–0. Even the regimental history mentions the dinner that followed, at which the 2nd Battalion 'was entertained royally'. Grandfather describes it as 'a somewhat hectic night', after which he seems glad to have had a quiet horse to ride back.

Diary

July 22nd. In Buire. Sleep and rest.

We all, I think, felt somewhat depressed and tired, having lost most of our friends in one fell swoop.

July 23rd. Go to church. Take over Bombers. See Doctor.

I went to church because I felt that I should, in a seemly manner, offer up some words of thanks to the Almighty for being allowed to still live, when so many better men had been killed. I took over the Bombers because I was told to do so. The Colonel I believe thought it somewhat of a compliment to me; why, I never quite understood. The Bombers were always called 'the suicide club'. They were chosen from that element of the Battalion that the Americans would term as 'rough necks'. They were however a very decent lot of men and I liked them.

July 25th. Still in Buire. Organise Bombers. Ride with
   MacFee 4 p.m.

MacFee was the transport officer and a rather wild
Canadian.

July 27th. In Buire. Ride 5 p.m.

July 28th. Inspected by General.

July 30th. Go to Church. Presentation of medals by
   General Langdon. Ride 5.30 p.m. Jock.

Jock, I remember, was a very rough horse and by no
means a comfortable ride.

July 31st. Ride Dundee 5.30 p.m. Fine and warm.

August 1st. Ride Jock 5.30 p.m.

August 2nd. Bathe 4 p.m. Ride Jock 5.30 p.m.

August 3rd. Ride Peter 10.30 a.m. and again 5.30 p.m.
   Wood comes to dinner. Lecture by R.F.C. Captain.

Wood was the Quartermaster and looked the part.

August 4th. Lecture on Gas.

August 5th. Ride Jock 5.30 p.m.

August 6th. Leave Buire 10.10 a.m. Camp at Bécordel
1 p.m.

August 7th. In Bécordel. Working party to Mametz
2 p.m. Return 9 p.m.

We were engaged in digging a trench through Mametz
village, or rather where the village had been. There was
a little shelling but not much. The place had been cleaned
up a lot since we had last been there.

August 10th. Still in Bécordel.

August 12th. In Bécordel. Move to other side of
railway.

In Bécordel we were in rough huts and bivouacs. Why
the whole Battalion was moved to the other side of the
railway, a distance of only about 200 yards, I never
understood.

August 13th. Go to Church of Scotland service.

August 14th. Working party leaves 6 p.m.

August 15th. Return from front line 4 a.m.

These working parties were no pleasure parties. They generally entailed either carrying bombs or ammunitions from the reserve to the front line, or digging new trenches in 'no man's land', or re-digging communication trenches that had been destroyed by gun fire and that frequently were again destroyed before we had even finished them. The whole time we were of course either being shelled or expecting to be shelled.

August 16th. Leave for front line 3 a.m.

August 17th. In front line.

It will be seen that after the short rest that followed the attack on High Wood the Battalion was back in the thick of it again.

August 18th. Prepare to leave 2 p.m. Leave 6 p.m. Lie south of Mametz Wood 10 p.m. Leave for front line east of High Wood.

This constant moving from one part of the front line to another was no joke as the communication trenches were generally unhealthier than the front line. The first part of the line we had been sent to on the east of High Wood was practically denuded of defending troops. The troops that had been there had made an attack and nearly all had been wiped out. We were expecting a counter attack, which fortunately did not come off. Whilst we were there some of the troops that had made the attack crawled back, most of them wounded. We had patrols out all night and helped to bring back a lot of the wounded. The dead we never bothered about.

August 19th. Leave front line 4 p.m. Go to trenches north of Bezantine le Grand (*Bazentin-le-Grand*).

August 20th. In trenches north of Bezantine le Grand. Fair amount of shelling.

August 21st. In same place.

In these trenches north of Bezantine le Grand we had very little to do; they were not bad trenches, but had no dugouts. The weather was rather wet and the only place to lie down was in the trench. We used to hollow out sort of slabs at the side of the trenches and hang waterproof sheets over them. We could get plenty of waterproof sheets from the dead. It was very cold at dawn but we used to have a rum issue at that time which put life and warmth into us. I always took a very good tot of rum and then lay down feeling like a giant refreshed and had two or three hours' good sleep.

August 22nd. Leave trenches north of Bezantine le Grand and go to High Wood. Hill and Scott go sick. Take over 'C' Company.

Hill was a regular and O.C. Company; he had been getting worse for some days. He had shell shock and nervous break-down; used to wake me up in the night and ask if I was hit and where the shells were exploding. Scott was, I think, the other Company officer.

August 23rd. Miller hit in right shoulder. Smart joins 'C' Company.

Miller was the remaining officer in 'C' Company. It was surprising how quickly our officers were disposed of. They did not last more than a few weeks and even less on the Somme front. I do not seem to remember Smart; he must have been killed or wounded very soon. The front line in High Wood was then only about 20 yards from the German front line.

August 24th. Line attacked on left and right of High Wood. Smart and Kennedy on patrol. German patrol fired on.

We were expecting a Boche attack at any time. We should have been in a bad way if the Boche attack on our right and left had been successful. The Boche could not very well shell our front line as their own front line was so very near ours. We shelled them but some of our shells landed in our own lines.

August 25th. German patrol bombed. Rifle Grenade strafe.

Our patrols and theirs were very active. We had men out on patrol every night. It was a hard job as the lines were so very close. There was grave danger of us firing on our own patrols. Being so near, the troops were a bit nervy, and rather too inclined to open fire without making sure who they were firing at.

As I was O.C. Company I did not go out into 'no man's land' so often as I had in the past. 'No man's land' was simply covered with dead. One dead officer in particular lay just in the middle between the two front lines. He had on a wrist watch, field glasses, etc. He was surrounded with our dead and I had a shrewd suspicion that the Boche had a rifle trained on that spot and used to fire on it at intervals during the night. Several men wanted to go out and see who it was. What they really wanted was the wrist watch and glasses, etc. I pointed out the danger, and forbade anyone to go near him. I do not think that we had anyone killed or wounded whilst on patrol, but all the time we were having people hit in our front line.

The Rifle Grenade strafe was a very good example of the advantages of retaliation. The Boche started firing trench bombs at us every few minutes. At first I did not take much notice as all the bombs were going over us and doing no harm. At last one landed in our front line and killed a man in my old platoon whom I knew well. I was much annoyed and sent a runner with instructions to the other three platoons that every time the Boche sent over a bomb they were to reply with a volley of four Rifle Grenades. These were to be fired by the bombing section I had organised in each platoon. The Rifle Grenade was a bomb that was fired from a rifle, with a long iron shaft that went down the barrel of the rifle. The Boche, when they found that for every bomb they sent over they got four in return, soon stopped. We then, just to close the discussion, sent over a volley of four from each platoon. We had evidently fired well and done them some damage as we heard a lot of commotion in their lines. So my old friend in No. 10 platoon was I hope revenged.

August 26th. Leave High Wood for trenches north of Bezantine le Grand.

In High Wood I had made my Company headquarters in a hole that was about four feet deeper than the trench.

This hole was being used by the R.E.s who were using a machine worked like a pump to give hydraulic pressure. It bored a small tunnel with a diameter of about six inches. This tunnel was to be under 'no man's land' into the Boche front line. As it was bored tubes of an explosive called, I think, ammonite were forced into the tunnel.

The idea was to eventually blow up this tunnel and so make in one moment a rough communication trench through 'no man's land' right up to the Boche front line. At the same time an attack was to be made which would be much helped first by the moral effect of the explosion and secondly by having the communication trench ready made for supplies to come up to us when we occupied the Boche lines. The idea was very good but unfortunately one of our patrols reported a steel bar moving on the surface of 'no man's land'. There was no apparent reason for it to move and they came back rather concerned and frightened by something they could not understand. This was reported to the R.E.s who discovered that it was their own blessed boring apparatus that had been deflected by some stone and had come to the surface. They remarked that they wondered why the work had become so much easier, as they had found the pumping business not nearly so hard to do.

The flies (house flies) in this part of the line at that time were a perfect plague. They covered everything. In this same Company headquarters dug-out they were massed on the ceiling like a swarm of bees. These flies made it very difficult to eat as they covered the food one was going to put into one's mouth. I was fortunate in having muslin net I put over my head when resting. They were filthy, fat, dirty flies that used to swarm round the dead. I had a great loathing for them. When a man was asleep they would settle all round his mouth and over his face.

August 27th. In trenches south of Bezantine le Grand.
Leave for trench on Mametz Hill. Very wet dug-out.

This latter dug-out was cut out of soft sandstone and all the time water was trickling down the sides and oozing up from the floor. Whilst here we received our parcel post mail. Very strangely I and another officer both received a tin of shortbread from the same shop in Glasgow; evidently both sent off at the same time by different people. Mine was from my then future wife. Living in a soaking wet dug-out we never got dry. The weather was wet and beastly, and, although August, cold.

August 28th. In trench on Mametz Hill. Very wet and damp.

August 29th. Leave for trench by side of Fricourt Wood. Wet night. Thunderstorm.

I forget if we were all very lousy at this time; we were all certainly very wet. The wet weather however had one advantage, and that was that the shells were not nearly so dangerous; they generally buried their noses before they exploded and most of the splinters went upwards.

August 30th. Same place; raining all day.

August 31st. Same place. Leave 7.30 a.m. March all day. Have fever and dysentery.

And no wonder!

September 1st. Stop in some village; go straight to bed.

Whilst on the march I was unable to get on my horse and had to be pushed up by my men. When up I could not get down; an awkward predicament when suffering from dysentery. When we got to the village I lay down and someone, hearing me groaning, fetched the doctor. Very many men were ill in the same way.

September 2nd. Am taken to 29th Casualty Clearing Station in ambulance 8 a.m.

September 3rd. Leave 29th C.C.S. Am put in train.

September 4th. Arrive No. 8 General Hospital Rouen.

The C.C.S. was composed of tents. No. 8 General Hospital was a collection of huts.

September 5th. In hospital.

There were some bad cases in my ward. One man came in with a bad hand and arm wound; his blood was poisoned. He was slightly delirious and all the time kept on singing 'Oh, you beautiful doll, you great big beautiful doll', a favourite song in London at the time. Men that were dying had a screen put round them. The nurses were over-worked and some of them I thought rather hard in disposition. The doctors were splendid fellows but they also were overworked. All the C.C.S. and hospitals were crammed full, and they hurried the patients out as soon as they possibly could. In this way many cases with only slight wounds were sent home to England as there were so many bad cases that could not be moved. Dysentery cases for obvious reasons were not suitable to go by train and boat. Many cases with bad wounds that could not stand being jolted were put on long strings of barges on the river and sent down to the coast by that means. They were then taken directly off the barges into the boat that took them over the Channel and then kept in hospitals at the English ports.

September 10th. Put clothes on for first time.

I seem to have been in bed for ten days, but the first few days I was asleep most of the time and half asleep for the rest of the time, making up arrears.

September 11th. See Walter. Visit Rouen town.

This was Walter MacGuire, a very old friend, in fact my oldest. He was in the A.S.C.

September 12th. Leave No. 8 General, go to 21st I.B.D. Go down town in evening.

September 13th. Leave 21st I.B.D. Go to Etaples (*Étaples*).

September 14th. Arrive Etaples 6 a.m. breakfast Station Hotel: very bad coffee. 3 p.m. go to Paris Plage. Dine Etaples Club.

September 15th. In Etaples take three drafts for 33rd Division.

A poor job, taking drafts. Hours in the train; sometimes days on end. Picking up bits of food when possible at wayside stations, men getting lost; sometimes having to change trains at all hours of the night; often stopping in some siding for hours on end. No job for a man just out of a sick bed.

September 16th. In train. Arrive Le Bret, hand over drafts to guides. Go to see 1st Battalion at Pommier. Stay night there.

It was rather lucky having to take drafts to my own division as it enabled me to call on my own battalion.

September 17th. Walk over to see C.O. at Brigade Headquarters. Walk to station: catch train at 6 p.m. for Abbeville.

September 18th. Spend early hours of morn in Abbeville. Arrive Etaples 8 a.m.

September 19th. In Etaples.

September 20th. Go to Paris Plage afternoon and evening.

September 23rd. Go Sports, and Duchess of Westminster's Concert in evening.

The Duchess of Westminster was supposed to be running the Duchess of Westminster Hospital in Paris Plage. At the Concert she was acting with a Jew called Lewis. I believe she afterwards married the man. I thought he was a growth.

September 24th. Go to church in morning to hear Millar. Paris Plage in afternoon. Leave for 1st Battalion at 8 p.m.

Millar was very well known for preaching extraordinarily good sermons. His Church was always packed.

September 25th. In train. Arrive rail head 6 p.m. Stay night with MacFee.

September 26th. Go billeting at St Armand. Battalion arrives 12 p.m.

September 27th. In St Armand, take charge of Company. Apply for leave.

I forget how I came to apply for leave, but expect I must have missed my turn whilst I was in hospital. It was a mistake to be backward in asking; I never made a mistake of that sort. Others yes – leave no.

September 28th. Strafe about leave. Pay out. Kit inspection.

September 29th. In St Armand.

September 30th. March to Lucheux: arrive 10.30 a.m.
Good billets and mess. Ride to Doullens.

It was in Lucheux, I think, that we were able to get a
wonderfully good natural aerated water, very good to take
with whisky; we had to pay for it.

October 1st. In Lucheux. Conference by Divisional
General Pinney.

The conference was about an attack we were going to
make on a wood half way up a long slope. After I had
been up the line to examine the line of attack through
my glasses I came to the conclusion that there would be
a hell of a slaughter (of us) and that the attack would be
a failure. The distance was too great and the Boche wire
very thick and heavy. All this time I was still persisting in
my attempts to get leave. I was told that if I waited till
after the attack I should get two weeks' leave but that if
I went before I should only get four days as I must be
back for the attack. What a hope!

I was reasonably certain that if I did not go before the
attack I should never go at all. Also I did not forget that
half a loaf was better than no bread. I was therefore still
keener on getting leave even if it was only for four days.

Also if I got leave I intended to make the best of it, as I could picture that attack up the long slope, through thick wire and under heavy fire. The wood in spite of being called Nightingale did not conjure up in my mind any sweet singing birds and I knew that if we ever got there the only whistling we should hear would be the whistling of bullets. General Pinney was always very keen on making attacks, a damn sight too keen in fact. The troops always said that he had a glass of blood and cream every day before breakfast!

October 6th. Still in Lucheux. Hill visits trenches.

October 7th. I visit trenches.

October 8th. Practice attack. March 11 miles.

The attack was practised by having an exact plan made, on a large open space, of ours and the Boche trench system, this plan being made possible by aerial photographs. We were formed up in our trenches as we would be 'on the night of the party' and then proceeded to walk over and rout the imaginary enemy. All very nice and easy, and according to Cocker. The eleven mile march was a part of the training to make us fit for the slaughter.

'Oct 9th 1916. Many thanks for letter recd. ¼ hour ago.
Very sorry to hear the Guv [his father] is not very fit. Have
just retd from a visit to the trenches and investigation of
the ground in front thereof. Beastly weather here.'

October 10th. See Colonel re leave.

The previous day was my birthday. I evidently had no celebration.

October 11th. Leave Lucheux for Doullens: walk all the way with heavy pack. Get leave papers. Leave Doullens 4.30 p.m.

October 12th. Arrive London 4 p.m. Turkish Bath R.A.C. Sleep Richmond.

October 13th. See Guv and Uncle. Take Tommy to Empire: dine Piccadilly.

October 14th. Dine Stillmans 8 p.m. Will and Laure. Take Rita to *Potash and Perlmutter*. Tea at Savoy.

October 15th. Lunch with Princes at Reigate. Supper Rita and Nora Pyrland Cottage.

October 16th. Lunch Faggs. See Mrs Slocombe. Dine Pyrland. Go to Gaiety Supper Savoy with Rita.

October 17th. See Guv and Uncle. Lunch Pyrland. Call Faggs: see Duke. Dine Hatchetts – Maudie, Tommy and Jessica. See *High Jinks*. Sleep Grosvenor.

A leave train arrives at Victoria station.

October 18th. Leave Victoria 7.50 a.m. Rita sees me off. Breakfast Pavilion Hotel, Folkestone. Leave Folkestone 3.5 (*sic*) p.m.; arrive Bologne 4.45 p.m.

And so ended my short leave and even now my heart sinks as I think of it. It was a pitiable sight to see the women left on the platform as the train went out.

October 19th. Arrive Bouquitmaison 10 a.m. Find Battalion has moved. Hang about village waiting for train. Train arrives 6 p.m. Leave 8 p.m.

October 20th. Arrive Abbeville 2 a.m., wait in luggage room. Go to hotel 7 a.m. Stay there all day. Leave Abbeville 9 p.m.

The time trains took to get anywhere was almost incredible.

October 21st. In train pass Poix at 10 a.m. Arrive Maricourt 5 p.m. Feed at canteen. Sleep Divisional Headquarters.

October 22nd. Leave for Citadel. Arrive there 1 p.m. Find Battalion has left. Reach Battalion 6 p.m. Take over 'C' Company.

October 23rd. Leave for Guillemont 7 a.m. Arrive
8 a.m. Stay night there: raining.

Guillemont had once been a village. It was then a muddy
flat covered in bricks. The only things that showed that
at one time it had been inhabited were broken iron
bedsteads and their springs, and tin pots such as are generally
kept under the aforementioned beds.

October 24th. Lie in open at Guillemont.

The last bath I had had was before I left London on October
17th. Some time during my journey I had picked up a few
lice, evidently a few more had taken a fancy to me in
Guillemont, and I was rapidly getting very lousy. I do not
think that I got rid of those lice until my next leave.

October 25th. Same place.

October 27th. Move up to trenches opposite Le
Transloy. Guide loses his way. No. 10 Platoon wander
about most of the night. End up with 'B' Company.

The whole place was a wilderness. The trenches, where
there were any, much broken down and inches deep in
water. All the ground was very exposed and each platoon
had to go up separately.

I, with my Company Headquarters, had a separate guide. We met No. 10 Platoon whose guide had also lost his way in the mud. The two guides then joined forces in the hopes that they might do better together. Between them they kept us wandering about all night. We were lucky in finding even 'B' Company. I was rather concerned as it looked bad for a Company Commander to have lost all his Company bar one platoon. Also I had with me the Company sergeant major and the signallers. For all I knew the other three platoons had walked right into the Boche line.

October 28th. In trenches by Le Boeuf (*Lesboeufs*). Five killed, six wounded. Sergeant Dyer badly wounded. I find 'C' Company about 10 a.m.

The casualties were due to shell fire. I expect we made such a noise swearing our way through the mud and water that the Boche thought we were going to attack them and asked for artillery support.

This part of the line was up to then the worst in which I had been. I refer more particularly to the mud and water. All the land had been very churned up by shell explosions, and for many days the weather had been wet. It was not possible to dig for more than about a foot without coming to water. Mud is a bad description as the soil was more like a thick slime than mud. When walking one sank several inches in and owing to the suction it was difficult

A pack-horse laden with trench boots.

to withdraw the feet. The consequence was that men who were standing still or sitting down got embedded in the slime and were unable to extricate themselves. As the trenches were so shallow men had to stay where they were all day. Most of the night we had to spend digging and pulling men out of the mud. It was only the legs that got stuck; the body being lighter and larger lay on the surface. To dig a man out the only way was to put duck boards on each side of him and then work at one leg, digging, poking, and pulling, until the suction was relieved.

Then a strong pull by three or four men would get one leg out and work would be begun on the other. Back to Battalion Headquarters was about 800 yards. At night it would take a 'runner' about two hours to get there. Going to and from Battalion Headquarters from the line one would hear men who had missed their way and got stuck in the mud calling out for help that often could not be sent to them. It would be useless for only one or two men to go to help them, and practically all the troops were in the front line and had of course to stay there. All the time the Boche dropped shells promiscuously about the place. He who had a corpse to stand or sit on was lucky.

October 29th. In trenches. 'D' Company attack; move
  up to reinforce 'B' Company.

The attack was naturally a dead failure. What else could be expected? We had only about 50 yards to cover from our front line to the Boche front line, but to cover that 50 yards through the mud would take nearly five minutes during which time the Boche would quietly pick off our men at his leisure. Those of 'D' Company who got more than a few yards were killed or wounded. Some of them never succeeded in getting out of our trenches.

It was madness to attempt the attack. It could only have been instigated by a higher command that had simply looked at a map, put down a finger and said 'We will attack there'. They could not possibly have had the faintest conception of what conditions were like in that part of the line where the attack was to be made. As I said above, even to get out of the trench was extremely difficult, let alone to cross 'no man's land', quite apart from enemy rifle and machine gun fire.

I had to take 'C' Company up over the top to reinforce 'B' Company, the idea being to assist in repelling any counter attack the Boche might make. The Boche were not such damn fools as to attempt to leave their front line. Those of 'D' Company who were not killed crawled back that night. After and during the attack the Boche shelled us a bit, but owing to the soft ground did little harm.

Extract from letter dated October 29th:

'Am sitting in a hole dug in the side of a trench 5 feet by 3 feet with a board stuck up in the middle to help support the roof. At present there are two of us in here; later on I shall try to get my other officer in. It is raining and thick mud is at the bottom of the hole; outside in the trench the mud is about a foot deep and in many places up to one's knees. Across the entrance to this hole is hung a torn waterproof sheet covered in mud on each side; a heavy bombardment is going on and this place continually vibrates as the Boche is using big shells.

Mud on the Somme: 'more like thick slime'.

'My putties (*sic.*) and boots cannot be seen for the mud they are covered with, in fact I am one mass of mud from head to foot. I have got on a man's overcoat that on account of the mud must weigh about 50lbs; round my neck is a muddy sodden Balaclava helmet that I have put my head right through. I have not shaved for three days nor have I taken off my clothes since I left England; I am itching a lot and my feet are wet. I have lost twelve very good men owing to a big shell exploding in the trench. I have a blister on my left heel. Saw two men blown up 30 feet in the air this morning, one coming down entire. We made an attack this morning at day-break; cannot get any food cooked: rather expect a counter attack tonight, but have just smoked a good cigarette; your pipe is drawing well and I am feeling in consequence in remarkably good form but am rather worried about that question of "how do you get your trousers on".'

October 30th. Lyn goes sick. Leave trenches, relieved by 9th H.L.I. Leave 12 midnight. Terrible march back, very tired, rheumatism. Hail and heavy rain.

I shall never forget that march back. Pitch dark and every step a labour and pain. Hail cutting our faces, bitter cold and soaked to the skin. My rheumatism was in my shoulders, where my heavy harness dragged on me. All our clothes etc. were extra heavy owing to being soaking wet and covered with mud. Besides a very heavy waterproof I had hung on to me a large revolver, about 20 rounds of ammunition, steel helmet, compass in leather case, field glasses in case, case containing a large number of sodden maps, haversack and contents, a gas mask in case. The mud on us alone must have been a great weight. As we dragged our way out of the trenches we heard men on each side of the path we took, shouting out for someone for God's sake to come and dig them out of the mud. Poor devils, some of them must have become exhausted and been drowned in it. I should have loved to have gone round and given them all a good tot of the rum that the 'Christian gentlemen' at home (blast them!) thought was so bad for the troops to have.

October 31st. Arrive Briquitre at 5 a.m. Raining hard. Take on Laws as servant.

November 1st. Tea at hospital. Rain.

November 2nd. Ride over to see Will. Back at 5.30 p.m.

Will being my brother, Dr W. H. Stewart, a Captain in the R.A.M.C.

November 3rd. Move 800 yards.

November 4th. Same place. Beastly wet.

November 5th. Leave 3 a.m. March to Fleurs (*Flers*)
Line, take over from 5th S.R. Rest. Carrying party 5
p.m. Big strafe.

In the part of the line we were then in we had quite good
deep dug-outs. They were, I am almost sure, old German
dug-outs. The entrances faced towards the enemy. Our
dug-outs were not dug that way as there was more risk
of a shell coming down through the opening if it was
facing the direction from which the shells were coming.

I have a drawing, done on a page from a field service
note book, of the dug-out we were in on the above date.
It was done by Stanley Cursiter, a well known artist and
one of my Company officers. At the time of writing he
is the Curator of the Royal Academy, Edinburgh. I very
much prize this drawing. It is typical of many other dug-
outs I was in. It shows the boarded up ceiling; the plain
earth floor; the steps leading up to the trench; on the third
step of which a coal and coke fire is burning in an old
tin. On the left of the steps two old petrol tins containing
drinking water that always tasted of a mixture of petrol
and chloride of lime; trench coats and tin helmets hanging
up on the walls; also equipment and revolvers in their

cases; on the right a candle stuck on to a piece of wood driven into the clay wall of the dug-out; on the floor boxes of bombs and ammunition, and tin plates with knives and forks.

The reason for the fire being on the steps was to let the smoke escape better and to help to ventilate the dug-out, also that the man doing the cooking, such as it was, would have more room. With several people in the dug-out the atmosphere soon got very warm and thick; most likely the inhabitants had not had their clothes off for days or weeks.

A spade can also be seen on the left. All dug-outs were supposed to have a spade left in them in case any part fell in, so that the occupants might be able to dig themselves out, if they were lucky.

November 6th. Same place. See Vivian Grey and
   others of 2nd Battalion.

I had no idea the 2nd Battalion were taking over from us, and the first intimation I had was Grey with his great voice shouting down the entrance to the dug-out: 'Does anyone know where that old ***** Stiffy is?', to which I replied in appropriate terms.

Why he always called me Stiffy I know not. It was an offensive term. At one time at Nigg I used to play a lot of poker with him. He was a very good chap; he had had a brother of whom he was very fond killed. In consequence he was very anxious to bayonet some Boche. At a later date he had much pleasure in having his desire gratified. He was a very big strong man, and came from Australia.

November 7th. Leave Fleurs line for Carnot. Arrive 10 p.m.

November 8th. Leave Carnot 10 a.m. for Muilte (*Méaulte*). Arrive 1.30 p.m.

November 9th. Fine day. A rare occurrence.

Extract from letter dated November 9th:

'I have got on a new pair of riding breeches and washed my hands for the first time since October 19th . . . Notwithstanding the best efforts on the part of the gentle Hun the bells did not ring for me. Two or three times daily they strafed all round the hole in the trench I was in, with 5.9's and 9.2's but except for making themselves very offensive to my ear drums and about fifteen times covering me with mud thrown up by their beastly shells, they put me to no further indignity . . . the mud in parts of the line here is terrible in places; it took me half an hour to go 100 yards. I am very much annoyed by memos sent round from Headquarters that come in at all hours of the day and night; they stop me getting a full night's rest and some of them are very silly and quite unnecessary. When I am very tired and just getting off to sleep with cold feet in comes an orderly with a chit asking how many pairs of socks my company had a week ago; I reply 141 and a half. I then go to sleep; back comes a memo: 'please explain at once how you come to be deficient of one sock'. I reply 'man lost his leg'. That's how we make the Huns sit up.'

November 11th. Leave Muilte at 9 a.m. for Buire Station; train starts 12 noon. All day in train.

November 12th. Arrive Citerne 5 a.m. Have breakfast 6 a.m. To bed; get up at 1.30 p.m.

November 13th. In Citerne billeted at Curé's.

This village of Citerne was a long way behind the line and a very restful and quite pleasant place. My Company Headquarters was in the house of the Curé, a charming old gentleman and just that type of good French village priest that one reads about in books; no money and no leisure and his only pleasure to minister to his flock; an old man – he looked about 75. We often conversed on the war, he speaking French and I English. We neither understood each other but he seemed to much enjoy the conversation. Several times I invited him to dinner with us, told everyone they must be on their best behaviour, and gave him a very good dinner and plenty of drinks. We had got plenty of food and all sorts of drinks from a canteen in some town near us, and were doing ourselves very well. The old man did so enjoy the drinks, loved the liqueurs, and became quite festive; in the ordinary way he was a sad old man. He used to retire fairly early saying something about taking mass early in the morning. Out of politeness, I think, he would have his last drink about a quarter of an hour before he left and most of this quarter of an hour he would spend thanking us and saying: 'non, non, merci, non' as we offered him 'just a little more'. A charming old gentleman; we liked him and he liked us. He was most unhappy when we left.

November 16th. Am supposed to take over bombers from —.

The reason for this was that I had to hand 'C' Company over to an old regular officer. As I almost invariably took command of the Company when we went into the line and into action the Colonel and the new Company Commander did not quite like putting me into a subordinate position every time we came back out of the line, hence the subterfuge of making me O.C. Bombers. As a matter of fact I used to do more or less what I liked, and used to do anything the O.C. Company for the time being wanted me to do. Some tact was required as the regular officers thought I might kick at only having the Company when they were in action and in a way thought it rather hard on me, and at the same time they on their part did not like never being sent with the Company when we went into the trenches. They were all very good chaps and sometimes used to try and explain their mixed feelings in the matter and apologise to me because, as they said, I had all the dirty work.

As a matter of fact this arrangement suited me down to the ground, as I was saved all the bother and trouble of filling in forms and answering questions from Battalion Headquarters at all hours of the day and night when we were in rest, and yet always had command of the Company when there was anything doing. From High Wood onwards I was always O.C. Company when the Battalion was not behind the line, except of course when I was away from the Battalion. Also even when we were in rest and I had handed the Company over to someone else my pride was flattered because I always believed that the men looked upon me as the 'big noise'. Also I always had considerable say in the training and no responsibility.

November 17th. Ride to Abbeville; get back 4.30
 having left Citerne at 7 a.m. Nearly frozen.

161 ABBEVILLE. — Rue Saint-Vulfran. — LL.

'It is most beastly cold. Survived last night. Froze most of the day.'

ABBEVILLE. — Le Pont des Prés. ND. Phot.

'This pic is like one of the Thames'.

November 18th. Prosecute in court-martial in Abbeville.

November 19th. 'D' Company beat 'C' 3–1. Alston goes on leave.

'D' Company beat us at football. I lost money on bets.

November 20th. Ride over to 20th R.F.

November 22nd. Divisional football 1st v 20th R.F. Hunter goes on leave.

Hunter was the O.C. Company; a regular, and a very good chap.

November 23rd. Racing at 20th R.F.

November 25th. Big boxing show at Citerne.

November 26th. Ride over and find out where Will is and lunch with 2nd Battalion.

That is our second Battalion, the 2nd Scottish Rifles.

November 27th. On court-martial 2nd R.W.F.

Extract from letter dated November 27th:

'Did I ever tell you that the last time we were in the trenches I was the last Company on the right of all the British armies on the Western Front and was in touch with the Frenchie's left.

A distinction, what?'

November 30th. Dine with 2nd Battalion. Play 2nd Battalion at football: beaten 5–0.

A somewhat hectic night. I rode back but had a quiet horse. It was bitter cold.

December 2nd. Pontifex and Grey dine with 'C' Company.

Pontifex was an old friend of mine at Nigg. He was an R.C. and a very nice chap indeed; very religious. The R.C. priest at Nigg had given Pontifex and me little charms to carry, with an engraving of the Virgin Mary on them. He said they would help to keep us from harm; a jovial little chap he was, that priest.

Pontifex still carried his and I think carried one or two more: they made him happier. I had lost mine. Pontifex was killed the next time he went into the line. He was a good chap and brave; I am sure that for him fighting went very much against the grain. We had a splendid time that night he and Grey dined with us; many a joke and much laughter.

December 5th. Firing on range,

December 6th. Dine at Headquarters.

December 7th. Colonel goes on leave. Hyde Smith returns.

December 8th. Leave Citerne 6 a.m. by train. Arrive Vaux sur Somme. Sleep night in billet.

December 9th. Arrive Camp 111 at 5.30 p.m. Sleep in hut.

December 10th. In Camp 111.

December 11th. Leave Camp 111; go to camp 20. Arrive at 2.30 p.m.

These camps were a collection of huts arranged in fields of mud in geometrical order. Duck boards were generally laid down to prevent people slipping and to make inter-communication easier. The huts were fairly dry and windproof, and sometimes had rough beds in them on which we could lay out our valises.

December 12th. Ride up towards trenches.

This was done in order to have a better idea of the way if we suddenly had to go up to the line in the dark.

December 13th. I ride up to the line.

December 14th. Battalion moves up to front line 10 p.m. I go to front line 3 a.m. Spend day in reserve line.

December 15th. In front line.

December 16th. Left front line 11 p.m. Go to Reserve line.

December 17th. In reserve line.

December 18th. Leave reserve line 6 p.m. Go to Brigade support line. Stay night with M.G. Captain.

I have no recollection of why I seemed to have moved my lodging every night. Most likely the front line was under enemy observation so that no one could move during daylight. This would mean that men had to stay quiet in the mud all day getting frozen and trench feet; hence the necessity for a change of location every day.

December 19th. Leave Battalion 11 a.m. Go to dug-out near brigade in Le Foret (*La Forêt*). Brodie takes working party.

December 20th. Near Le Foret.

December 21st. Same place.

December 22nd. Leave Le Foret at 4.30 p.m. Arrive Camp 17 7.30 p.m. Wire bed, a great luxury.

December 24th. Pay out. G.O.C. inspects huts.

December 25th. In Camp 21.

December 26th. Leave Camp 21 at 10.45. Arrive Camp 13 2 p.m.

December 27th. Leave Camp 13 at 12 noon for Edge Hill station. Leave by train 5.30 p.m. Arrive Eaucourt 10 p.m.

December 28th. Billeted in farm by river. Have large room all officers sleep in mess.

Am quite unable to remember the place.

December 29th. In Eaucourt. Kit inspection. Hourston goes to Abbyville (*Abbeville*).

December 30th. In Eaucourt. Laws paid to date.

And so ended 1916 in the happy knowledge that the first seven years of a war were always the worst.

A Bloody Spring

French propaganda postcard.

JANUARY 1917 saw my grandfather at the Fourth Army School at Flixécourt. The lecture on bayonet fighting which he enjoys has been memorably described by Siegfried Sassoon, who was there the previous year:

The star turn in the schoolroom was a massive sandy-haired Highland Major whose subject was 'The Spirit of the Bayonet' . . . He spoke with homicidal eloquence, keeping the game alive with genial and well-judged jokes. He had a sergeant to assist him . . . trained to such a pitch of frightfulness that at a moment's notice he could divest himself of all semblance of humanity. With rifle and bayonet he illustrated the Major's ferocious aphorisms, including facial expression. When told to 'put on the killing face', he did so, combining it with an ultra-vindictive attitude . . . Man, it seemed, had been created to jab the life out of Germans. To hear the Major talk, one might have thought that he did it himself every day before breakfast. His final words were: 'Remember that every Boche you fellows kill is a point scored to our side; every Boche you kill brings victory one minute nearer and shortens the war by one minute. Kill them! Kill them! There's only one good Boche, and that's a dead one!'

My grandfather would soon need all his 'fighting spirit', because a new 'push' was in the works. The Allied strategic situation remained unpalatable. The sacrifices of 1916 had borne little fruit. Russia was now visibly tottering and desperately in need of support. Indeed, the Tsar's regime collapsed in March 1917. Clearly, a new offensive on the Western Front was required. This was no less obvious to the Germans, however, who in February and March withdrew from the vulnerable salient opposite the Somme battlefield, straightened their line to free up reserves, and fell back to defences they had prepared on the so-called 'Hindenburg Line'. This move dislocated the original Allied plans for another combined Anglo-French joint offensive. Instead, the new French commander, Nivelle, who thought he had discovered a new method to unlock the German defence within forty-eight hours, proposed to attack on the Chemin des Dames ridge, south-east of Laon, in April. Haig would assault first, at Arras, to draw German reserves away from the French.

420 GUERRE_1914-1915. — Arras — Le travail des Sauvages (les Allemands) après leurs bombardements.
The Savage's work (the Germen) after their bombardments. — LL.

Again, early British successes could not be exploited. On the first day, 9 April, the Canadians stormed Vimy Ridge and the British centre progressed 3½ miles: further than any Western Front advance of the war to date. Thereafter, however, the limits of First World War communications, and the difficulty of moving men, artillery and supplies over a shattered battlefield, caused the attack to lose momentum. The British could 'break in' to the German defences, but did not yet have the means to 'break through'. The battle degenerated into a series of bloody thrusts making ever less progress.

The original strategic purpose of the battle of Arras soon evaporated. Nivelle's offensive of 16 April was a failure, with nearly 100,000 casualties in the first week, and it was soon clear that no grandiose Allied pincer movement would be possible. By the middle of May, fighting on the Chemin des Dames had petered out. A series of complaints about harsh conditions in the French army escalated into a wave of limited military 'strikes', leaving the French temporarily incapable of taking fresh offensive action.

In this environment, the British had to maintain what pressure they could on the Germans. By now, also, Haig was planning a new onslaught in Flanders, from which he wished to distract enemy attention as best he could. Thus, British attacks near Arras went on. In terms of casualties per day, the Battle of Arras became, in fact, the bloodiest ever fought by the British on the Western Front.

The Cameronians had been repeatedly involved from mid-April onwards, but my grandfather was not initially engaged. Having been ill, he was first sent on convalescent leave, and then left behind the lines, with the 'B Echelon', as part of the group of officers and men regularly held back from major actions to provide a cadre on which the battalion could be rebuilt if necessary.

He did, however, rejoin the main body in time to attack Tunnel Trench in the second line of German defence, the Hindenburg Support Line, on 27 May. By this stage, after six weeks of near-continuous fighting, the battalion was down to six officers and 350 men. The initial attack, as he describes, was successful, and they took the enemy trench. He seems unclear as to what then went wrong. Things often do misfire in battle for no clear reason. On this occasion it appears that 'B' Company went too far forward, was hit by friendly artillery, and then came under heavy German fire. When they fell back, the rest of the battalion followed. The attack had failed; Colonel Chaplin took the blame in the inquest that followed. My grandfather, however, emerged well. He was awarded the Military Cross, according to his citation, 'for conspicuous gallantry and devotion to duty in leading an assault into the enemy's trench. He knocked out a hostile machine gun, personally killing and wounding most of the team, and throughout the attack he handled his company with marked skill and courage'.

Diary

ON THIS first day of January 1928 I start the second part of my short War story, today being exactly eleven years after that day of which the first entry to follow treats.

My experiences during 1917 were little different from those during the greater part of the preceding year. After nine months more or less intensive warfare I considered myself a veteran and had, I think, with the exception of the Colonel, seen more war service than any of the other officers in the battalion. I had certainly learnt how to look after myself and the men under me. Mistakes could not often be made more than once.

So far as I was concerned I found that as the months passed by, one's natural subconscious fear of death or injury was less easily held subservient to one's will or true personality. This was particularly the case at dawn or during very cold weather.

At dawn a tot of rum was a great help (I said tot not a lot) which leads me to believe that the expression

'Dutch courage' is a misnomer and 'in vino veritas est' a true saying. But as one who has read my diary and comments for 1916 tells me that I have already said more than enough about rum and the lack of it, I will continue my diary for 1917.

January 1st 1917. Still with Battalion at Eaucourt.

Extract from letter dated January 1st:

'Tonight I am having the pipers in to play at dinner so will then drink your very good health again. Am feeling somewhat fed up today owing, I think, to the constant stream of chits which come in from Headquarters asking damn fool questions at all hours of the day and night; for example last night at 11.45 a chit came round asking for a list of piano tuners and photographers in my company. I sometimes wish I had never had the damn company . . . The last trenches I was in were the worst I had ever been in, which is saying a lot. Since joining this battalion I have done more days in the trenches and seen more fighting than any other officer here, so think I deserve the five weeks out I hope to get.'

January 3rd. Leave Eaucourt and go to 4th Army School in Flexicourt (*Flixécourt*). Arrive 12 noon.

This school at Flexicourt was situated in a small town of that name. The course lasted for about six weeks. It served the double purpose of giving some of the infantry a rest from the front line and at the same time giving them very useful instructions in their duties. The course consisted of drill, bayonet fighting and lectures on all subjects. One of the best lectures was given by a Col. Campbell on the fighting spirit and bayonet fighting in particular. Col. Kentish was in command of the school.

I had quite a good billet with a French family: a room to myself with a comfortable bed and a small stove in which I generally had to burn wood. Coal was very scarce and even wood was very difficult to get. The weather was bitterly cold most of the time and there were some heavy falls of snow.

We were always kept fairly busy all day and sometimes in the evenings, but I enjoyed my stay there and having a bed to sleep in. I could also get a bath one or two days a week and consequently I expect got rid of my lice.

January 4th. In Flexicourt. Lecture by Gen. Kentish.

This was the first lecture of the course and we were all told the things we must not do and the things we were expected to do. Kentish was afterwards in command of the senior officers school at a place near Aldershot.

The course continued the even tenor of its way and my next few entries are of little interest.

January 7th. Go to Amiens.

January 20th. Still at Flexicourt. Go for day to Amiens, return 11 p.m.

Cathédrale d'AMIENS — L'Ange Pleureur de Blasset

'Jan 22nd 1917. This is the kind of thing I go into Amiens to see.'

173

Nothing much to do in Amiens except to have drinks in a well-known American Bar, have one's hair cut, and look in the shops.

February 10th. Course ends. Leave Flexicourt 6 p.m. Arrive Souzanne (*Suzanne*) 11 p.m. Sleep night Div. H.Q.

Div. H.Q. was in a large French Chateau that was somewhat the worse for wear. It was bitterly cold. I remember I was very glad to sleep in a large room with a big fire. The room was used by the signallers and was very crowded.

February 11th. Leave Div. H.Q. 3 p.m. Arrive Curlu 5 p.m. Join transport; sleep night in transport lines.

Once again I was back with my Battalion, again on the move and sleeping (sometimes) in a different place most nights. Curlu was a place on the Somme. The river there seemed to spread itself out into a large number of smallish channels. It was at the time frozen over, but in most places the ice could not be walked on. The transport was housed in dug-outs and bivouacs along the bank on some rising ground on the left side of the stream. The river was crossed by pontoons and small foot bridges. They were I think very seldom shelled. The dug-outs had rough wire bunks in them.

February 12th. Orders to go up to front line. Arrive
Reserve line 4 p.m. Take over 'D' Coy. from
Walker. Go up to front line 9 p.m. Take over from
20th R.F.

I rather fancy that Walker had only been with the Battalion
a short time, anyhow I do not remember him at all well.
This was the first time I had ever been away from my
own company and I was very sorry to leave them. One
of the regular officers was in command of 'C'.

February 14th. Walker wounded in face.

Owing to the hardness of the ground the shell fire was
much more dangerous and I expect that there were a good
many more casualties that I do not mention.

Walker was hit in the eye but not knocked out; he said
it was painful but not very bad. As he had lost his coat I
gave him the fleece lining to my trench coat. He was sent
home. I never saw him or my lovely fleece lining again and
the weather was bitterly cold. However, I would rather that
he had my fleece lining than that I should have his eye.

Extract from letter dated February 22nd:

'Damn, the post has been closed for 4 days and worse
still I hear that all leave is stopped for 6 months . . .

took away my fleece lining by mistake and left me with nothing to keep me warm at night; I was not quite frozen to death but very nearly. Fortunately the following day I got back the wounded man's flea bag; like everything else on the Somme now, it is lousy but it kept me warm and a few lice one way or the other don't make much difference. How would you like to be lousy; if you like I will enclose a few in my next letter . . . The mud is now as bad as ever it was.

'. . . We have been issued with a new box respirator. When in the alert position one has to wear it strung just under one's face like a nose-bag, but some of the men were glad to have them last time we were in the trenches as the Boche put over some gas bombs and shells. I got one or two sniffs of it myself but nothing to hurt. The dug-out in which I now sleep is very damp, water runs down the walls and falls off the roof but I louse and frouse and suffer no ill effects.'

February 15th. Hourston on patrol. Gas shells sent over, am ill in the morning.

I nearly died. I thought I had been gassed but had not. I was suffering from carbon monoxide poisoning. This was the way of it, the dug-out was made as follows:

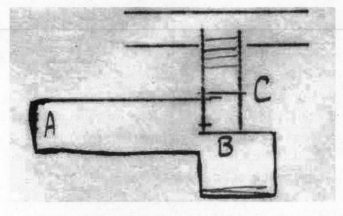

We were all very cold so started a good coke fire going
in an old tin: this was placed at 'B'. To try and stop the
draught we hung an old blanket at 'C'. The dug-out sloped
down from 'B' to 'A'. I slept on the ground at 'A'. The
others slept at round about 'B'. No ventilation; coke fumes
finding the lowest level. Result they had some difficulty
in awaking me for 'stand to' at dawn when they knew I
would want to go round the trenches. When they did
wake me I thought I was dying but managed to crawl up
into the trench, where I was violently sick and so continued
for some time. My head was almost more than I could
bear. The freezing air and the sickness made me better in
time, but everyone thought I had been badly gassed. Some
of the others in the dug-out were affected but to nothing
like the extent that I was.

February 16th. Frost ends. Are relieved by the 20th
  R.F. Go back to Howitzer Wood.

When the ground was frozen there was more danger from
shells owing to them exploding the instant they touched
the ground. When the thaw set in we were knee deep
or deeper in mud and movement was very difficult. I
don't know which was the worse. It depended I suppose
on the amount of shelling we experienced.

February 17th. In Howitzer Wood; arrive 2 a.m.

My memory of many of the places we were in during
1917 is not so good as for 1916. I was I suppose becoming
a bit war weary and took less interest in my ever changing
location.

February 18th. In Howitzer Wood; leave for Transport.
  Sleep 'B' Echelon

February 19th. Take bombing class 23 men.

February 20th. Dine with Town Major; Curlu.

This was not a dinner party. The Town Major had a hole
in a tank boarded round with odd bits of wood etc. The
'town' consisted of similar 'houses'. The Town Major was

an officer appointed to tell incoming troops where they should go and to see that the place was kept in good order and clean. A very 'cushy' job.

February 21st. Fire Rifle Grenades in afternoon.
Brown returns from leave.

February 22nd. Ride to Maricourt; see Will.

February 25th. Leave 'B' Esch (*sic*) Curlu, go to Camp 19; arrive 2 p.m. Battalion arrives 3 a.m. on 26th.
Ride over to see Will who is ill in bed.

February 26th. In Camp 19.

February 27th. Ride over to see Will; 15 Corps Hosp. Maricourt.

March 1st. Fine day. Company training starts.

All Battalions that were back from the line for a rest were kept busy doing intensive training in preparation for the Spring Offensive of 1917.

March 3rd. Still in Camp 19 Suzanne.

March 4th. 8th Division go over the top 6.30 a.m.

Our 2nd Battalion was in the 8th Div and many of them were known to us. From where we were we could see the strafe and the barrage our guns put up and also the Boche counter barrage. The shelling from both sides was very heavy.

March 5th. Take over 'D' Coy. Go up to Clery
  Chateau just north of Somme. Take over from
  Queens 8 p.m.

March 6th. In same place.

I have not much recollection of this part of the line. My mind must have become dulled owing to the very many parts of the line in which I had been. All I can remember is that our line ran right down to the banks of the Somme and we were told tales of men having swum from one line to the other.

March 7th. Leave trenches; spend night in Camp 19
  Souzanne.

March 8th. Leave Camp 19 for Camp 12. Arrive 12
  noon.

March 9th. Arrive Camp 12 near Corbie. Beastly place.
  Get fever; go to bed.

Dinner in the snowy trenches, March 1917.

The Camp was I think on a hill and it was bitter cold. I remember little else except the cold and that it was a desolate place.

March 10th. In Camp 12. Bad fever; stay in bed.

March 11th. Fever better: get up 1.30 p.m.

March 12th. Still in beastly hole Camp 12.

March 14th. Fever again.

March 15th. Get up 11 a.m. Fever again, take over 'C' Coy.

I seem to have had a lot of fever, but remember nothing whatsoever about it. The 'bed' I lay in was I expect my valise laid out on the ground.

March 16th. Reorganize 'C' Coy.

March 17th. See plane fall to ground. Phillip rejoins company.

A nice boy Phillip. Very young. He was killed before very long. We used to play cards together. When he was killed I had a cheque of his for a hundred francs or so. I paid it in some weeks after his death and it was met; I do not know how this was. Anyhow he would have been disappointed not to have paid his gambling debts. A very nice chap, always wore his tin helmet very much on one side of his head.

March 18th. Ride over to Corbie.

March 19th. Still in Camp 13.

March 24th. Leave for Amiens 5.30 p.m. arrive 6.30
p.m. Dine Gobart. Leave Amiens 12 midnight.

The Gobart was the best place for dinner in Amiens but
very expensive. The food after army rations was wonderful,
and some of the waitresses charming.

March 25th. Arrive Boulogne 2.30 p.m. Sleep Officers
Club.

I managed to get a bed but many spent the night on the
floor or in chairs in the sitting rooms. My diary seems to
have become very sketchy as no previous mention is made
of this apparently sudden departure for leave. In fact I
wrote little and seem to remember less. I must have been
full of fever and muzzy in the head.

March 26th. Boat leaves 12.15. Arrive Folkestone
2 p.m. Arrive Victoria 4.20 p.m. Arrive Richmond
7 p.m. Sleep Richmond.

I was staying in Richmond with my brother Tommy and
his wife Jessica.

March 27th. Call Macdonalds 4 p.m. Meet Tommy
7 p.m. Hatchets.

The Macdonalds were my future in-laws; they then lived in 8 Prince of Wales Terrace, Hyde Park.

March 28th. Take Rita to Gaiety. Lunch Pyrland.

March 29th. Dine Pyrland. Rita, Hutchie, Lunch Guv. 1.30 p.m.

March 30th. Dine Mrs Lumley-Cook. Theatre.

March 31st. Dine Macdonalds. Go to theatre.

April 3rd. Go to War Office. Lunch Scotts. Call for Rita p.m. Go to Harrods.

I had been spending most of my leave in bed with fever and very painful rheumatism and went to the War Office to see if I could get an extension of my leave on account of sickness. Harry Wadd had given me a letter to take to the War Office. They granted me extra leave and the result was:

April 5th. Leave with Macdonalds for Slapton by car 11 a.m. Arrive Andover lunch 2.30 p.m. Arrive Honiton 7.30 p.m. Dine and sleep. Very good hotel.

The next day we must have arrived at Slapton, where Tommy and Jessica were and there we stayed until:

April 15th. Arrive Pyrland at 7.30 p.m. Have tea
Hatton Hill. Meet Will. Lunch at Newbury.

April 16th. Go to War Office. Chu Chin Chow with
Rita and Tommy.

April 17th. Leave Victoria 7.45 a.m. Arrive Folkestone.
Leave by boat 7.45 p.m. Arrive Boulogne 10 p.m.
Sleep Hotel Maurice.

Another tour in France survived and another leave over.
I could hardly expect to come back again unless sent home
wounded. All on the boat for France hoped to return
whole but few would expect to do so.

April 18th. Leave Boulogne 1.45. Arrive Abbeville
5 p.m. Lunch Officers Club. Dine ditto. Leave
Abbeville 12.30 midnight.

April 19th. Arrive St. Pol 6.30 a.m. Sleep night
Officers Rest House.

April 20th. Try to rejoin Battalion; fail. Lunch
Doullens. Leave St. Pol 1.30 p.m. Arrive Doullens
4.30 p.m. Sleep night Hotel Quatre Filles Airen.

Extract from postcard dated April 20th:

'Am still wandering about France, may come to rest tomorrow. The Battalion has been in action. See Casualty List. Have to report to you with reference to German prisoner on Station platform.'

The story of the German prisoner was that on one of the platforms on which I was waiting there was also a very inoffensive German soldier in the charge of a British private. A long train slowly passed through the station, the first half being full of English troops. At every window there were one or more men looking out. They took little or no notice of the German, except that a few called out 'What cheer Jerry', 'Blimey ain't 'e lucky' and other remarks of a similar nature.

The second half of the train was full of French troops, each window as before having one or more occupants, but every Frenchman as he passed the German shouted out some offensive remark at him, meanwhile shaking his fist. This continued till nearly the last carriage arrived and then one Frenchman who thought he knew English and wanted to say something original shouted out 'You blady bustard' much to the amusement of all.

April 21st. Unable to get any trains. Leave Doullens by car 7.30 p.m. Arrive 'B' Echelon 10 p.m. Sleep there.

'Vive la sporte.'

Along the bottom edge of the card my grandfather has added *'to keep as pets'* after *'Searching for German lice'*.

Five days it took me to get there, most of the time in trains, or waiting for trains, and expecting to be cussed for being so late in rejoining my Battalion. Very often trains would come into a station but no one would know where they were going to. It was also sometimes very difficult to find out where one's Battalion was, particularly when it was on the move. Food I would get when I could. Sleep I took when I felt inclined to it. To prepare for sleep I found a sheltered nook and lay me down. As I had rid myself of lice whilst on leave, I was fairly clean and not troubled by being lousy, but fleas were very prevalent in France. Personally I would rather have lice than fleas. I generally had both.

April 22nd. In 'B' Echelon.

Extract from letter dated April 22nd:

'I at last came to rest with the Battalion last night and heard all the news. The man who gave me the flask of good brandy has been killed. The man, my C.S.M., for whom I got the pipe has been badly wounded, also the officer to whom I was sending some things from Fortnum and Mason, also the man who I told you was a T.T. and non-smoker, also others of whom you do not know.

I am now billeted in a broken down place that I think used to be a stable. To get here I had to pass

through many places that had once been villages but
had been razed to the ground by the Germans before
they were driven out. Behind where our line used to
be are many trees, but over here not one is to be seen,
everyone having been sawn down by the Boche. Near
here is the place where the village crucifix was, as usual
surrounded by about a dozen trees in a mound. All
these have been cut down, also the cross which now
lies on its back.

The people of France will have things to remind them
of the war for the next hundred years.'

April 23rd. At 'B' Ech. Big attack 5 a.m. Walk up to
see Battalion.

April 24th. At 'B' Ech. Germans retire. Go up to
Hindenburg line 3 p.m. return 2 a.m.

I do not know why these frequent visits to the line. Working parties I expect. I happen to remember the above visit
because it was my first to the Hindenburg line; a wide,
deep, very well-made series of trenches. This trench had
only just been captured and was thick with German dead;
ours had been buried or removed.

The party I had taken up contained many boys, just
out in France, who had seen no fighting. The sight of so

many dead men was upsetting them and I was joking and chaffing them, trying to buck them up by telling them the old joke about a dead German being a good one. One dead man I covered up because he was such a nasty sight and bad for the young troops' morale. There certainly were a lot of dead about in that trench.

Extract from letter dated April 25th:

'Yesterday I spent most of the day in a certain German line of which you have read a lot in the papers. Got back here 2.30 this morning. Had the pleasure of seeing a large number of German dead lying about the trench.'

April 25th. 'B' Esch. Move to tent. Battalion comes out of the line.

April 26th. March to tents, spend day there. Take over 'B' Coy. from Hogg.

Little Hogg who was one of my Coy. officers is now a full blown Major.

April 27th. March to Baillerval (*Bailleulval*); arrive 12.30 p.m. In billets.

April 28th. In Baillerval, cottage catches on fire.

We were very crowded in Baillerval, five or six of us sleeping and living in one small room.

April 29th. Hunter takes over company.

Hunter was a regular and a very nice chap; he had been wounded earlier in the war.

April 30th. McLellan dines with 'C' Coy. On Court of Enquiry 6 p.m. Gen. Pinney conference 4 p.m.

The conference was I expect about some attack. Pinney was very keen on that sort of thing.

May 2nd. Leave Baillerval 2 p.m. Arrive Monchy, a ruined village, 5 p.m.

May 3rd. In Monchy. Very fine weather.

May 4th. In Monchy. Very fine weather.

May 5th. In Monchy.

May 6th. In Monchy.

Extract from letter dated May 5th:

'I am at present sitting on the top of a large pile of bricks that once used to be a house. The weather continues excellent. There are three triplanes overhead playing about like a lot of puppies, turning somersaults, etc.'

May 7th. Div. Race Meeting.

A very good show and some quite good sport. I see by my cash account for that day that I lost forty francs over sweepstakes.

May 8th. Raining hard.

Extract from letter dated May 8th:

'I spent a part of this afternoon walking about the old no-man's-land and inspecting ours and the German lines; very interesting. I rode over to the races yesterday and back in the cool of the evening, on my way there going through several ruined villages. On the wall outside one of them was the name of the village with the word "Late" placed before it; only too true: one can hardly tell they were villages.'

May 9th. Fire on range.

May 10th. Brigade scheme. Go for ride 4.30 p.m. Still in Monchy.

May 12th. Leave Monchy. March to Boisieux (*Boisleux*) St. Marc. Tommy has operation.

Ten days we rested in Monchy. This was about the longest 'rest' I can remember. We were evidently being fattened up for the 1917 Spring Offensive. A long rest was always followed by a thick time in the trenches.

May 13th. Still in Boisieux St. Marc.

May 14th. Still in Boisieux St. Marc.

May 15th. Take R.E. working party. Leave Boisieux St. Marc. Go to 'B' Ech at Moyenville (*Moyenneville*).

May 16th. In Moyenville.

Extract from letter dated May 16th:

'It has been rather cold today; (strafe just started) and is now raining. I am in a cellar in which we have got four bunks, quite a nice place. The strafe is spreading: I wonder what it is all about.'

May 17th. In Moyenville.

May 18th. Batt. comes out and goes to St. Ledger (*St Léger*) 11 p.m.

When I went to 'B' Echelon the Battalion had evidently gone into the line without me. No one seems to have been killed so I suppose they did not have very much to do.

May 20th. Batt. attacks at 7.30 p.m. Hindenburg line. Scott and Oppy killed. Take carrying party up 10.30. Scott killed. Murie wounded.

There were two Scotts, officers in the Battalion. Murie was I think in my Company. We were taking up bombs and ammunition in anticipation of a counter attack that did not come off I am glad to say. It was never much fun being with a carrying party going up to the trenches after an attack, as the enemy were in a nervous state and did a lot of shelling and machine gun firing in consequence. Also one never knew when one might be let in for a bloody counter attack. The day was Sunday; we generally seemed to attack on a Sunday. Our visit was not a pleasant Sunday outing.

Extract from letter dated May 20th:

'A show came off this morning, and another one is coming off in 31 minutes time. I am not in it. The pioneers have been making nice white crosses today, they are before me as I write; hope my name will not be placed upon any of them. What I can not understand is how the people at home stick these blasted strikers. They should all be placed under military law and then if they still played the fool shot. And I should like to have the job of doing it.'

It will be seen that the crosses mentioned in the letter were needed. My comments on the strikers in good safe jobs at home (which comments were made in France at the time) are now of interest.

May 21st. Still at Moyenville. Leave Moyenville 10.30
 p.m. Join Batt. at St. Ledger. Take over Coy.

May 22nd. Batt. arrives 2 a.m. Phillips dies of wounds.
 In St. Ledger.

Phillips was a very nice boy. I used to gamble with him. I was very sorry when he died. He can not have been more than about 19 years old.

Extract from letter dated May 22nd:

'Left the place where I was somewhat hurriedly. Just by this place are a lot of big guns that are making a Hell of a row and shaking the whole place. Lot of strafing going on here.'

In this letter I am also urgently asking for naphtha balls that I wanted to try and keep my lice under control.

May 23rd. Still at St. Ledger. Cheques to Bank.

May 24th. In St. Ledger.

May 25th. Go up to front line to see the lie of the ground.

We were still lying in St. Ledger in bivouacs and huts; doing very little and having quite a restful and pleasant time as the weather was warm and fairly fine. Whilst in this place we got a lot of revolver ammunition and after some practice about five or six of us had a sweepstake, on who could hit the top of a cigarette tin the most times at about five paces' distance. Five paces does not sound far away but is a good distance to fire at a small object with a revolver. We had six shots each and although we all got very near we made few actual hits. I won the stakes with I think two hits. I had a very good, accurate, long revolver which was a great help. Before many days I was extremely glad to have had this chance practice and to have gained the confidence I had in my ability to shoot straight. I knew that if I could hit the top of a cigarette tin two times out of six I could hit a man's head eleven times out of twelve.

Revolver bullets are made out of uncovered soft lead and expand when they hit anything. Rifle bullets are made out of lead covered with nickel and go slick through that which they hit, except at very close range when they make a bigger wound.

May 26th. Group to Hindenburg front line. Put Coy. out into shell-holes in 'no man's land' at night.

We went up to the front line as soon as it was dark. The whole Battalion being in the line. Each Company occupied a frontage of about 150 yards. I had 'A' Coy. on my left and on my right I think 'D' Coy.

Our instructions were that as soon as it was dark to send out strong patrols into 'no man's land' to see that the coast was clear and that then the whole Company was to go out and occupy a position about fifty or maybe one hundred yards in front of the front line. The Company was to be extended out in as straight a line as possible, the men making themselves as comfortable as they could in shell-holes.

Each platoon had to cover about forty yards of the front. I told the platoon officers to get as near to the centre of their platoons as they could and to put their platoon sergeant on the flank. Every one was told that no noise was to be made and that there was to be no swearing or talking.

To get the Company out in the desired order does not sound a very difficult operation, but I had 'had some before' and expected the worst. I got all the platoon officers and platoon sergeants together and explained to them in detail everything that had to be done. They were told to all start out together having first sorted themselves out into their right order in the front line trench. From which trench they would advance in extended order for fifty yards and then halt, get into the nearest shell-hole and lie down.

We were not actually in the Hindenburg front line but in a small trench that had been dug about 15 yards on our front of it. This, as it afterwards turned out, was very fortunate. When all the men of the Battalion were out in the desired position they were to stay there till zero hour, the time of the attack.

We expected to have everything in order some hours before dawn. The general idea was to have the whole Battalion out in 'no man's land' as near to the Boche as they could be without being detected, that they should stay there till 1.55 the following afternoon. At that time all our artillery, both big and small guns, were to open a very heavy barrage on the German front line and about twenty yards on our side of their front line. A part of 'no man's land' was included in the barrage in case the Boche had any advanced posts. The time 1.55 p.m. was chosen because it was known that after their midday meal it was the custom of these Boche to retire into their dug-outs, take off their equipment and go to sleep. They had been left in peace for some time, and would never expect a sudden attack in broad daylight.

The Boche had a habit of sending over low-flying aeroplanes every morning to examine our lines and to see if we were doing anything special. For this reason all our men that were to lie out in 'no man's land' had been repeatedly told that they must on no account turn their faces up when the aeroplanes came over, as if they did so they would most likely give the whole show away.

After the above explanatory digressions I will return to my narrative. As mentioned it sounded fairly easy to get the Company out into the desired position but I expected the worst. When they were all sorted out in the trench I sent them off 'over the top' having again told them the number of paces they had to go; each platoon being under its own officer. They were told to go quietly and not to hurry as they had all the night before them. Off they went in good order and without much noise. It was a pitch black night. After a minute or two some of them started swearing, so off I had to go falling in and out of shell-holes going along the line behind them and by dint of counter-swearing managed to more or less stop some of their foul language. I then left them and returning to our front line smoked a pipe.

Having finished my pipe I started off again from the extreme left of my front to see that all was in order. I found that the left flank of my left platoon was in touch with and level with the Company on our left; quite correct. I then paced out the distance that my left flank was from our front line. Then to the right that platoon and again pacing out the distance found that the right flank was too far back.

Leaving a man where their right flank man ought to be the platoon officer and I proceeded to get the platoon straight and on the right line, no easy task as it was difficult to find all the men in the dark. Also they had settled themselves in the very broken shell pitted ground and were loath to move. The same performance had to be gone through more or less with each of the four platoons. One platoon I remember was in a hopeless mess. A nervous young officer I expect who could not see in the dark. When I at last got to my right flank I found that the Company on my right were too far back; anyhow I said they were too far back, that we were right, and that they were leaving us 'in the air'. They moved up to my level. The officer in command of this Company was a very nice quiet chap, but rather nervous and with very little experience. I remember him very well but forget his name.

By the time everything was at last in order it was within an hour or so of dawn, so I started off again to go down the line and pass the time of day with all I came across. This meant sitting in endless shell-holes and cracking foolish jokes with the men. 'Mind you wake up when the barrage starts', 'I hope your bayonet is sharp' and so on. At last I got back to my Coy. H.Q. in the front line trench. My company H.Q. consisted of an officer I had kept back in case I was killed before the show started, my Coy. Sgt. Major, two runners and two men with a Lewis gun. I had a little cubby hole in the side of the trench and no doubt smoked a pipe and had a well earned sleep.

May 27th. Whit Sunday. In trench. Attack Hindenburg Support line 1.55 p.m. Forbes killed.

Before dawn I was pottering round the trench and sending off returns to Batt. H.Q. I also saw that the Lewis Gun was all ready to fire at the Boche plane that I expected to come over very shortly. Some time after sunrise when it was quite light the old aeroplane according to schedule appeared in the distance and I sent up a silent prayer that the men in 'no man's land' would remember to keep their faces down. I then got ready to send up a few bullets and went along to where the two men were with the Lewis

Gun. They were very keen to open fire but I told them to wait till I gave them the word. On came the plane flying very low. When it was over our front line it turned and started flying parallel with and over the trench in which we were. When it was nearly over the spot we were at I gave the word and the Lewis gun opened fire with a burst in splendid style. I and the others in another part of the trench blazed away with rifles. For a second or two the plane seemed to take no notice and then it suddenly banked and came towards us in a different direction. We continued to blaze away as rapidly as we could. We must I think have hit it as after about five seconds more flames came out from its exhaust and it rapidly turned and, still flying very low, hurried home – I hope much the worse for wear.

With that excitement over there was nothing to do but to wait for zero time. I had a book with me that for an obvious reason I was very anxious to finish before we went over the top. As the morning advanced it became very warm, everything was very quiet and there seemed to be no shelling in any part of the line.

As zero time drew near I saw that my revolver was loaded, a rifle also fully loaded with one in the breach and bayonet fixed slung over my shoulder, my gas mask in the alert position under my chin and my coat collar turned up and last, but by no means least, having seen that my pipe was going properly – I then at 1.45, ten minutes before zero time, went round to see that my small band of company headquarters were all ready for the trip.

My reason for turning up my coat collar was to make myself look as little like an officer as I could, it was also partly for this reason that I carried a rifle. Before any show started I was always very careful to see that my pipe was properly alight, as later there might not be the opportunity and I found tobacco a pleasant sedative. I am as I write smoking the self-same pipe which I have not smoked for very many months as I look upon it in the light of a mascot that must seldom be invoked. It was very inadvisable in an attack to be distinguished as an officer as the enemy were a damned sight too attentive to those who they thought were the leaders.

I found the men that were coming with me all ready and anxious in a way to be over the top and over the suspense of waiting for zero. I told them that immediately the first shot of the barrage was heard they were to follow me as we must hurry to come up with the rest of the company. I do not think that any of us were at all 'windy' but the last few moments before an attack when one rather expects to be killed or wounded are somewhat tense. As usual I suppose I made damn silly jokes, generally in very questionable taste.

As the minutes passed and we waited constantly looking at our watches, everything was unusually quiet and then – bang, bang, exactly at 1.55 over came two or three shells and we started to get 'over the top'; a fraction of a second later it sounded as if thousands of guns were firing over our heads with one deep loud roar; and where a second before all had been peace and quiet pandemonium raged. Personally I found the hellish uproar stimulating.

As I got on top of the parapet I saw all the Company about 75 yards in front of me, getting out of their shell-holes and slowly advancing in good order, at even distances between the men and in a fairly straight line. A hundred yards or more in front of them was a wall of smoke and bursting shells that could not be seen through. It certainly was a splendid barrage – very even and very dense. I hurried on as best I could to come up with the line and as the men had to advance slowly soon caught them up. It had been a hot bright morning and all the men had evidently been sleeping stretched out in the sun; they trudged on in and out of the shell-holes in a somnambulant indifferent manner but in excellent order. As I knew that no Boche could see through the barrage that was on and in front of their position I got on top of a little hillock to direct operations, to wave back those who were going too fast and to urge on those who were not far enough up, blowing a whistle that could be heard above the uproar to attract their attention. Those who did not think no doubt imagined that I was courageously exposing myself.

We continued slowly to advance until we were within about 20 yards of the barrage, which was like a wall before us. I did not see anyone hit by our shells although this sometimes happened when the barrage was so close. We had to halt for a few moments, until the barrage started to move forwards. This was always the critical time.

As the barrage moved I saw the whole of our line advance with it but right away to the left they were having some trouble with barbed wire. The barrage seemed to rest for a few seconds on the Boche trench and then like a live thing jumped forward about 50 yards. This was the psychological moment that the whole Battalion should have rushed forward and occupied the enemies' line. We tried to urge the men on but although none held back few hurried forward. Generally speaking they just meandered on in a sleepy manner. It was useless for me to attempt to influence any except those in my immediate neighbourhood, so with revolver in hand I pushed on knowing that those near would follow me into the trench and that others further down the line would follow in their own sweet time.

When I was within about five yards of the trench I saw a machine gun poke its nose over the parapet two or three yards to my left front so I moved obliquely towards it. I then saw the tin helmet of one of the machine gunners; at this helmet I fired with my revolver and do not think I can have missed. I then had a shot at a man who appeared the other side of the gun, I think I got him also. Then a head and neck appeared where the first man had been and

I had my third shot. Then some blighter in the trench just opposite me threw a stick bomb at us or me; it exploded just by my feet; he was a sitter and I got him also with my revolver. By this time things were happening a bit too rapidly to remain clear in my memory but there was one young chap I remember very clearly shooting in the back as he was running away but I forget whether I got him with a revolver or a rifle. My next recollection is that I had no more shots left in my revolver and was still not yet in the trench. As I had no intention of getting into the trench unarmed I proceeded to unsling the rifle with fixed bayonet I had over my shoulder. I should have mentioned that after my third or fourth shot I found that the bowl of my pipe and the smoke from it was obscuring my line of vision as I was firing slightly downwards all the time. Much to my annoyance I had to put my pipe in my pocket alight as it was; it was lucky that it did not burn my jacket.

Just as I got my rifle working I saw a man in the trench calmly kneeling down and taking careful aim at me; at the moment I saw him he fired but in some miraculous way he missed. It seems almost incredible that he should have missed at such close range; he was certainly not more than six yards away. Anyhow I did not miss him.

The next thing that I remember was being in the trench at last and someone was throwing bombs down into a dug-out that some Germans had run into; I have some faint recollection of a Boche appearing from behind the traverse where the machine gun was, but it is all very hazy. One of my officers called Smith, he was a Glasgow man, told me that he had been round to the machine gun emplacement, found all the team dead and had thrown the gun over the parapet, a very wise action that eventually may have saved many of our lives. I got into a corner and reloaded my revolver.

After a short time Smith came and told me that all our people had cleared off and that there were only Germans in the trench; after a few questions we decided that we also had better go back, so once again we got over the parapet but this time in the other direction. As the two of us got out of the trench we saw the whole blessed Battalion very slowly meandering back the way they had come, they were about a hundred yards in front of us. By their backs they looked fed up and although one or two Boche had by this time started to fire at them they made not the slightest effort to hurry or take cover. One episode I still have a vivid mental picture of because I suppose it impressed me at the time as being so funny. Away to my right I saw a Boche running after two or three of our men that were together, when he got up to them he caught hold of one of their jackets and waved his other arm, all the time following them. He was obviously asking to be taken prisoner. They however evidently did not want to be bothered with him and shaking their fists drove him away; he then scuttled like a rabbit back to his trench.

Smith and I walked hurriedly on but had not gone for more than ten yards before someone threw a bomb at us. Our situation was difficult. I knew that if we did not get into a shell-hole damn quick we stood a very fair chance of being shot in the back. On the other hand I knew that if we dropped into a shell-hole so near the trench the Boche would know just where we were and could spend the rest of the afternoon throwing bombs at the spot where we had gone to earth.

Neither of the two alternatives was in any way alluring, but the Boche at the moment were rattled and although we were very near we were not an easy mark as we were dodging in and out of shell-holes all the time. Having all the above in mind I immediately shouted out to Smith not to stop but to follow me, and crouching down I ran on until we came to a decent shell-hole at what I thought was the right distance. I think we were shot at as we ran but I am by no means certain. Into the shell-hole we dropped very out of breath with all the exercise we had been taking. We both had a well earned drink but we did not dare smoke for fear we should give away our position. We heard firing going on and a few bullets hit the edge of our shell-hole but no bullet could hit us where we were. With my knife I dug myself a seat in the side of the hole and made it a bit deeper. We were very

Battle of Arras, May 1917.

disgusted with the failure of the attack and could not understand why it *had* been a failure.

All of a sudden, to our horror, we heard a bomb explode behind us. It put the wind up me as I guessed they had seen about where we had taken cover and if I had not chosen the right distance or if they had a man who could throw a bomb a long way we might have one on top of us at any moment. I did not feel in the least inclined to risk making a rush for a shell-hole further away as the fact that some bullets had kicked up the dirt on the lip of our crater showed that they had rifles ready to fire at us with.

We decided to stick where we were and hope for the best, anyhow the bomb had landed some distance behind us. During the next few moments I felt more disturbed than at any other time of the day. A good many more bombs were thrown but the worst that happened was that once or twice their explosion sent some earth over us; and I felt more secure as I began to realise that we were just out of range. If I had not risked running those few extra yards in the first place those bombs would have been on top of us. As it was they were a long side too near to be pleasant.

Smith who was a very nice chap, and a stout fellow to boot, had only been in my Company a short time. He was a big and strong man and took up a lot of room in the shell-hole. I am not sure if he had been in France long but I think not.

He and I, after we had recovered from our fright with the bombs, discussed the situation which I thought was a bad one. I pointed out to him that the Boche knew where we were and that as soon as it was dark they would send out strong patrols to mop us up, and that if we tried to get away before it was dark we would be seen and likely be shot. We therefore decided on the following procedure. That we would start to tunnel out a wee trench to the next shell-hole. That as soon as the light began to fade we would worm our way through this little trench. That then we would follow the same procedure but more rapidly and with less care as it would not be so light and that from there onwards we would make our way back to our own front line separately, so as not to be so conspicuous. It was hard work making the wee trench as we only had our knives and our hands to do it with and we had to be careful to be quiet and not to show ourselves or the earth we had to dispose of. In the early twilight we chanced being seen and managed to get into the next shell-hole successfully. From there we made our way according to plan but I fancy that we kept together instead of separating. Nearer our line we heard voices and found the O.C. the company on my right who had also been stranded with another man in 'no man's land', but much nearer our own front line; he was slightly wounded: we then went on together.

Eventually we got back safely and I found all my company except a few that had been killed in the trench I had left at 1.55. One of my officers called Forbes had been killed, shot through the spine, some of the men had gone out and brought him in from 'no man's land' where he was lying in sight of our trench. Although he had only been dead about eight hours when I saw him he had already turned a bluish colour. I had seen this happen before but do not know the explanation.

After having made a bundle of all the things out of his pockets we buried him behind our front line. The men had certain rules that had to be observed when anyone was buried. The man's feet had to be towards the enemy

A battlefield burial.

and someone had to say some words from the burial service
and scatter a little dust over the body. I did not know
Forbes well as he had only been with us a short time.

I was very upset at the failure of our attack; so far as I
could see it should have been a great success. The men
were not in a good mood and very disgruntled with
their walk to and from the Boche line. I unfortunately
did not help matters by being for once in a way in a very
bad temper. I fully expected to be well 'told off' for our
lack of success.

213

The only thing that we could get out of the men was that the company on their left had never got into the Boche trench and that whilst some of my Company were fighting in the trench all the other company had started to retire, and seeing this they had done the same. Others said that they had been ordered to retire. At a conference that took place the next or following day it transpired that the left hand company were held up by barbed wire, that some of their officers were killed and that then some unknown person had shouted out an order to retire; it was allowed that they never entered the German trench.

After we had got back to our trench and when it became quite dark the Boche started a very heavy bombardment evidently expecting us to make another attack. Very fortunately for us they put their barrage down on the old front line where no one was and not on the line we were occupying which was about twenty yards in front of the old line. Whilst this barrage was on Smith did splendid work looking after some of the men who were a bit troublesome. The shelling continued more or less all night but although we had a few casualties owing to some shells landing short on account of bad shooting by the Germans, we did not suffer much harm.

At dawn the following morning the Brigadier General appeared in my trench and I prepared to receive my cursing for failure. I hurried up to him and told him that the trench he was in was exposed and dangerous, which was perfectly true, but I did rather stress the fact. He waited long enough to hear the little I could tell him, which was not much, as in all attacks one's outlook is very limited; he then went away as quickly as he could whilst I saluted smartly. I had met this General before and liked him, but he was a rather nervous man; nevertheless he would not have come up through all the shelling by himself to our advanced post unless he had been a stout-hearted fellow. If I remark anywhere that anyone is nervous I do not mean to infer that they are 'windy'.

I believe that the reason we failed to make good this attack was as follows. The men had been lying out all day up to 1.55 p.m. in a hot sun with no protection from its rays, they were tired and slept like logs. This made them sleepy and lethargic when they had to wake up and advance. The left company had some trouble with barbed wire, which difficulty they could have surmounted had they not been feeling so lazy; their officers went in front in an endeavour to hurry them on; when these officers were shot the men got fed up and simply would not take the bother to advance, then some ass shouted out 'Let's ***** well retire' and they did. The movement passed down the line and my men followed suit. What happened on my right I don't know; I never saw that company but hear they mucked it up, lost direction and went much too much to their right.

The failure of this attack made me very sick at heart.

May 26th. Return to Moyenville: arrive 12 midnight.
Go to Camp.

We all marched into the camp very disgruntled, sorry
for the good men we had lost, and also I think rather
ashamed of ourselves.

May 29th. In Moyenville. Brigade Conference.

May 30th. Same place. Pinney awards medals. Leave
for Bailleuval 3.45. Arrive at Bailleuval 6.30 p.m.

Pinney was the Div. General.

May 31st. In Bailleuval.

Extract from letter dated May 31st:

'Talking about poor devils, one of our officers had his
face blown away by a bomb; he lived for about an
hour.'

In Flanders Fields

PASSCHENDAELE, the popular name for the Third Battle of Ypres, remains today one of the most potent symbols of the Western Front. The very name evokes sacred suffering, and the miserable bog, through which the British and German armies had at times to fight, seems to encapsulate the horror and futility of war. The historian A. J. P. Taylor, for example, dismissed it as 'the blindest slaughter of a blind war'. This was to be my grandfather's next destination.

Haig's plan for the battle was to drive north-east from Ypres, scene already of two major battles and almost incessant small-scale fighting, capture the German rail junction at Roulers, and clear the Belgian coast of Germans. Liberating the ports of Ostend and Zeebrugge, which the Germans were using as submarine bases, would reduce the U-boat threat to British supplies and turn the German flank, restoring mobility to the war.

The ruins of Ypres in 1919.

The ruined town of Ypres lies in a shallow bowl, surrounded on three sides by gently sloping low hills. From their defences on top of these ridges, the Germans could observe every British movement in the salient below. The British generals were under no illusions that it would be anything but easy to break those defences. But Arras had shown that British tactical and technical innovations had opened up possibilities of progress, and confidence was high. Thus, once the British at Ypres had started to roll forward, an attack along the North Sea coast at Nieuwpoort would also begin, and, if sufficient progress was made, a specially trained division would make an amphibious assault landing, all working together to destroy the German position in Belgium.

The plan was, not for the first time, too ambitious. After a lengthy artillery bombardment, the attack began on 31 July 1917. Again, at first it was successful. Losses were heavy – some thirty thousand – but in several places the British had taken both the first and second lines of the German defence. Attempts to push on further, however, had been beaten back by German counter-attacks as the enemy used new 'defence in depth' tactics. A pause would be necessary before Haig could attack again, but by now rain was falling. It rained almost every day in August. Its drainage shattered by three years of shelling, the battlefield soon flooded, creating a giant marsh. In these conditions, it was impossible for the British to maintain the tempo of their offensive. Those attacks that were made in August were soon literally bogged down. The attacks planned at Nieuwpoort, and from the sea, were cancelled. Given my grandfather's description of conditions near the coast in his diary, this was a blessing.

In September, the British attempted a new approach. Instead of ambitious large-scale offensives, they would launch limited-objective attacks. They would nibble away at the German defences, using overwhelming power to capture ground but taking only what they were sure they could hold. The first of these new attacks was launched on 20 September along the Menin Road. The weather was dry, the ground actually dusty, and the attack was largely a success. Strongpoints that had stalled the British advance for six weeks fell, and German counter-attacks were repelled. Australian troops reached the edge of Polygon Wood, and began preparing another 'bite and hold' operation to take it. This attack was planned for 26 September. 33rd Division – Grandfather's – was to provide support.

As the division came up into the line on 25 September, however, the Germans launched a spoiling attack. This is the assault my grandfather vividly describes. It drove 33rd Division back and dislocated preparations for the next day. The Cameronians were sent up from reserve, into the line, to guard against further such attacks. My grandfather went with them.

Diary

June 2nd. Inspected by General Snow. Have a bath.

I did not often get a bath so it was worthy of note.

June 3rd. Go for ride with Hunter.

Hunter, as previously mentioned, was an old regular, who had been badly wounded with the Battalion in 1914. I generally handed the Company over to him when we came out of the line.

Extract from letter dated June 5th:

'By the way I never told you I was reported killed the other day; about six people swore that they had seen me lying out and were perfectly certain it was me.'

June 6th. Take over A Coy. Wright goes on leave.

Wright was the O.C. A Coy., a most amusing chap, his great remark was 'happy days' at appropriate and inappropriate times. He once killed an old Boche whom he should not have; I did not approve, but the way he told the story was very funny.

June 8th. Coy. attack and blocking a trench A Coy.

This must have been part of our training behind the line.

June 9th. Firing on range A Coy.

June 10th. Ride to field range with Hunter.

June 11th. Heavy rain all morn.

June 12th. Go in Bus from Adinfer Wood to Paris Plage. Leave 9 a.m. Arrive 6 p.m. Stay at Continental Hotel.

The Colonel decided that I needed a holiday, so sent me off to Paris Plage for a few days. I was not very keen on going as I knew no one there, and expected to be bored, which I was.

The Continental Hotel was on the front. It was quite pleasant to sleep between sheets far from the sound of the guns. Whilst with the Battalion we were seldom if ever far enough behind the line to escape the sound of

E. S. 1366 ░░░░░░░░ (P.-de-C.)
Hôtel Continental et Groupe de Chalets
face à la Mer

Stevigard, édit., Boulogne-sur-Mer

'Paris Plage, June 14th 1917. My room is marked with
a cross. I do not know who the girl on the chair is,
she is I believe waiting for someone'.

the continued firing. It was I think an old London bus
we went down on. I remember that I travelled on top
and had to continually duck to escape being hit by
branches of trees.

June 13th. In Paris Plage.

June 14th. In Paris Plage.

June 15th. Leave Paris Plage 1.30 p.m. Arrive Bailleval
8.30 p.m.

June 16th. Regimental Sports.

June 18th. Leave Bailleval 6.30. Arrive Moyenville 9.30.

June 19th. Go to B Echelon at Moyenville at 5 p.m. Sleep in cellar.

June 21st. Leave B Echelon and join 212nd F.C.R.E. at Moyenville. Hut to myself.

This was the 212nd Field Company Royal Engineers, they were working at clearing out a small stream and needed help. This should have been a nice quiet job for me but was rather spoilt by us being shelled sometimes. In the little valley where we were working was an enormous naval gun with a lot of machinery for getting the shell up. It only fired about once a week and not whilst I was there, but the Germans suspected it was somewhere in the valley hence the occasional shells. This was not a bad job and I had a bed of sorts to put my valise on.

June 22nd. With R.E. work on Sensée River at St. Ledger. Parade 6 a.m.

The Sensée was the small stream that had become blocked and that we were clearing.

June 23rd. Laws paid to date.

Laws was my servant.

June 24th. Same Job with R.E. Lunch with Hogg.

Hogg was a young regular officer who had been one of my platoon officers. A very good chap.

He had got a job as Town Major of some place and had made himself very comfortable indeed in a broken-down old house; he lived in the cellar, with the remains of the house on top of him.

When I went to see him he gave me a splendid dish of wild wood strawberries he had collected from somewhere; they were delicious. He was very bucked with the nice safe job he had got and said that practically no shells ever came over. I met him again a few days later and he was as sick as mud, because a time land-mine the Germans had left behind them had gone off very near to his cellar, and he was wondering if his cellar was mined. I heard later that other mines went up near the first one but none of them did him any damage.

Extract from letter dated June 25th:

'I now get up every morning at 4.45, start off at 6 a.m. and don't get back till the afternoon and am then so sleepy that I have to have a sleep, and before I know where I am the day is finished.'

June 28th. Rejoin Battalion 6 p.m. Take over C Coy.
 Take on McLennan.

I was not sorry to get back to the Battalion, as although the job I had been on was supposed to be a soft one I had been shelled with my party nearly every day. McLennan was my new servant; a stout-hearted red-headed fellow who feared nothing.

June 29th. Leave Moyenville 6 p.m. Go to Monchy;
 arrive 8.30 p.m. Billet in flooded cellar.

Monchy was a bad spot. A small village that had been razed to the ground. On account of the shelling we preferred to be underground even if the cellar was flooded. An officer of another company got a large tub and slept in it with his feet sticking out.

June 30th. On C.M. in Monchy.

C.M. = Court-martial.

July 1st. In Monchy.

July 2nd. Leave Monchy; march to Léalvillers; arrive 5 p.m., 12½ miles.

July 3rd. Leave Léalvillers 7 a.m. March 12 miles to Naours; arrive 1 p.m.

July 4th. Leave Naours 5 a.m. March 13 miles to Bourdon; arrive 11.30 a.m.

Twelve miles does not seem far for one day, but the soldier has to carry a heavy load with him.

July 5th. Leave Bourdon 5 a.m. Arrive Conde (*Condé-sur-l'Escaut*) 8 a.m.

July 6th. Ride with Hay 5.30 p.m.

July 7th. Draft arrives.

Extract from letter dated July 17th:

'I wonder if you can hear the guns going, even here we can hear them hammering away. Must say I am glad I am not any nearer them, they make my head ache after about 24 hours incessant noise. Also they blow one's candles out.'

2. HOSPICE DE BOURDON — Entrée principale

July 12th 1917. Never seem to get a moment to write nowadays.
Quite hot today. Tomorrow must be up at 4.30.'

NAOURS (Somme). — Mairie et Ecole.

July 14th. All leave is cancelled. Hell.'

July 18th. March to Horse Show.

Cannot explain the long break in my diary. Must have been fed up about leaves having been stopped.

July 20th. Batt. Boxing Show.

July 22nd. Weigh in Boxing 12 noon. Ride over to Aixaines.

July 23rd. Brig. Boxing. Ride over to Aixaines.

July 24th. Brig. Boxing finals.

Extract from letter dated July 26th:

'Leave is open but not for us poor devils; the A.S.C. seem to be the only people who get leave regularly and who least deserve it. They are very much looked down on by everyone out here, and know it and look it. The young ones I mean. Have got no news and am fed up about leave. Curse it.'

July 31st. Leave Conde for Bray Dunes 2 p.m.

August 1st. Arrive Bray Dunes.

Bray Dunes was a place on the sea just behind the front line. The part we were at was nothing but sand dunes and very much infested with flies.

August 2nd. Leave Bray Dunes 2 p.m.

August 3rd. Arrive Boulogne 12 midnight. Leave Boulogne 9 a.m. Arrive Folkestone 11 a.m.

Leave at last, which I spent in Bognor.

August 14th. Leave Bognor.

August 15th. Attend investiture.

By attending this investiture at Buckingham Palace I managed to wangle two or three extra days' leave.

August 16th. Leave London 7.35. Arrive Folkestone 9. Leave Folkestone 1.30 p.m. Arrive Bologne 3.30 p.m. Stay at 'Metropole'.

August 17th. Leave Bologne 5 p.m. Arrive Bray Dunes 10 p.m. Stay night there.

August 18th. Go up to transport lines. Return to camp in evening at Ghyvelde Bray Dunes.

August 19th. In same camp.

August 26th. Leave Depot Batt. Take 'C' Coy. to front line.

This so-called front line was the most extraordinary place that could be imagined. To start with no one quite knew where the front line was, and in any case the whole place was more or less under water. To get to the front we had to cross a fairly broad river or canal not very far from its mouth. The current normally when I was there ran at about the same rate as the Thames when the tide is coming in. This river was crossed by two very narrow plank bridges, the planks being lashed at intervals on to small floats. There was only just about room for two men to pass each other, and the whole contraption swayed in the current. These two bridges which were within sight of each other were generally being shelled, sometimes with H.E. and sometimes with shrapnel, the former being used in an attempt to smash the bridge or the moorings and the latter to kill those who were crossing. If the H.E. shells missed the bridge they did little harm as they generally exploded in the water.

If anyone were badly hit whilst on the bridge there was little chance for them, as the water was deep and to fall in when dressed for the trenches was to be drowned. Only a few men at a time were allowed to cross; consequently there was often some delay on the banks, particularly when the bridges broke away and went floating off as they sometimes did. During daylight the Boche often had the bridges under observation and would send over shrapnel if they saw anyone crossing; during the night the shelling was intermittent.

It will be seen that those who were on the Boche side of the river were in a very isolated position and stood little chance of much support in the event of being attacked. It was also very difficult to get rations and ammunition up to the line.

I have spoken of a front line, but there was in fact no line of trenches. The front was held by a series of 'posts'; one or half a platoon making the best they could out of water-logged shell-holes, and cellars if any. The country was quite flat and water was everywhere. It was not safe to move by day as the Boche had it under observation. The whole business was so chaotic that I cannot remember how my Company was disposed. I do know however that my Coy. H.Q. was in a shallow cellar half full of water and that I sent one platoon under an officer to take over a 'post' from a platoon that had made an abortive attack the night we arrived and had their officer, a man called Sussex, and several men killed. The bodies had been left in the mud. As we could only move about in the dark,

we were unable to gather much impression of the lie of the land as it all appeared to be the same, water, mud and shell-holes.

Soon after I arrived, I suppose about midnight, I received a written message telling me that I was at once to go up to the spot where we had just made the abortive attack and to examine the ground carefully, as the following night I had personally to lead an attack on the German post that was about 100 yards from our own. This is a nice game, thought I. They are not content with one officer getting killed, they now want another. After having been floundering in the mud I was a bit tired but as there were not many hours before daybreak, off I had to go taking my servant with me as an orderly.

It was not very far but wading through the mud in the dark takes a long time. I had a flash lamp but did not dare use it much, as the position we were in was so exposed and we might get near the Boche without knowing it. A part of our way was along the side of a canal; there was no bank, the sides being all smashed in. After we had gone about 100 yards the Boche started dropping big shells in and on each side of the canal fifty yards or so in front of us; we went on a little way and suddenly saw a big object on our left, half in the water. This turned out to be an old barge, and as a shell exploded very near us my man suggested taking shelter in it, but I would not do so as I said the Boche were probably taking the barge as their mark and might hit it. What with the shelling, the mud, and slipping into the canal it was a perfectly beastly trip.

As it was no good sticking where we were and time was passing, we pressed on. We passed a little cubby hole where I offered to leave the orderly, but he thought he ought to come on with me, so did. After much labour for what seemed like hours we at last arrived at our destination, a spot where the mud came nearly up to one's knees. Here I found a most miserable and woebegone collection of men and the officer; they were all squatting about in shell-holes wet to the skin and cold. What a jolly attack we shall have by the time tomorrow night comes, thought I, the poor beggars can hardly move now; what shall we all be like in 24 hours.

I asked what they had heard about the attack that had been made earlier in the night; they said that Sussex and the men that were killed had never got near the Boche and were still lying where they had fallen. The place where the Boche were was pointed out to me; they could not be seen but could be heard. I was told there were only about half a dozen of them and only about 100 yards away. To cheer our people up I told them I had orders to attack the Boche 'post' the following night. I then returned the way I had come and got back to my Coy. H.Q. at about break of day.

I then sent a written message to the Colonel saying that I had been to our 'post', seen where the German 'post' was, and that in my opinion there was not the remotest chance of the required attack being successful; or some few words to that effect.

I would here again point out the advantage I had over most of the regular officers, hardly any of whom would have dared to send a message of that nature. They would have acted on the principle 'theirs not to reason why' etc. Also they would have been very frightened of being thought afraid. Personally I did not care a damn what was thought, and knew better than anyone else that, unless there was some ulterior motive that made it expedient to sacrifice me and a few men, it was futile madness to make the attack. Needless to say if after having voiced my opinion I am again ordered to capture the German 'post' the attack comes off, and half the platoon comes with me.

About an hour or so after my message has been sent off by runner (a message about an attack could not be sent over the buzzer) an order comes through over the telephone line that I am to report to the Colonel at once at Batt. H.Q. Off I go, daylight by now, through the mud to the banks of the river and proceed to make my way along the edge to the bridge. Quite safe along the side of the river that I was on as the bank sheltered me from the shells which were only landing in the river or hitting the other bank. As I trudged along I saw that the bridge I had to cross was being shelled; men were scrambling over it as quickly as they could, one or two at a time. They generally waited till one shell had burst and then made a run for it hoping to get the other side before the next one came. Most of the shells coming over were shrapnel.

It was interesting to watch so I stopped for a rest by an Advanced R.A.M.C. First Aid Post that had been dug into the bank. It was most amusing to see the different procedure various men followed, some ran across the bridge as quickly as they could, some walked, others paused to watch the water; nobody was hit whilst I was watching and the bridge remained undamaged. In due course I also crossed in safety, and made my way to Batt. H.Q. only to find that the C.O. had gone to brigade H.Q. where I had to follow him.

Whilst I was at Batt. H.Q. the whole place was shaken by a very big explosion. I thought a mine had gone off but was told that it was a 15-inch delayed action shell the Boche were using with which they were searching for our Brigade H.Q. It appeared that they sent over three or four a day. I was told that they could do little harm as Brigade H.Q. was in a very deep old cellar, or dug-out, reinforced with very thick concrete. These shells went very deep into the ground and then exploded with such force that they made a crater like a small mine. I then went on to Brigade H.Q.

When I found the Colonel, he questioned me about my message with reference to the proposed attack. He said that he had had the order from Brigade. I told him that the Boche 'post' was in mud shell-holes the same as ours. The mud was about 6 to 12 inches deep, and that every movement in the mud could be heard a long distance on account of the squelching sound every time a step was taken. That from our 'post' to the Germans' would take at least 5 or 10 minutes to traverse, and that as we tried to walk the Boche would simply lie down and pick us off at their leisure. I finally suggested that the Brigadier, if he wanted the attack made, had better come up and see the conditions for himself, as it was quite obvious that he had not the faintest conception of the state of the ground where I had been during the night, and where the two 'posts' were. The Colonel, who understood, and had no more desire than I had to lose his men on damn fool stunts, quite agreed with me. He said that his orders were to make the attack; I must do my best; and made it must be, unless I received orders to the contrary. He then told me to go back and that he would see what he could do about it.

Whilst I had been waiting for the C.O. another of the 15-inch shells had come over and the whole cellar-dug-out had been shaken. These Brigade Headquarters were in a very large place like a labyrinth, and might have been cellars of a wine warehouse reinforced by us with concrete.

Before I left I went along to see if I could get any news out of any of the nice clean gilded staff, and found them in a great state of commotion as they were clearing out and going to some other place that was not being fired at. Although these big shells could not penetrate to the dug-out the concussion of them had caused several big cracks to appear in the concrete, and the staff had come to the conclusion that the place was not safe. I would not have minded swapping with them. My return journey was completed in safety and after telling the signallers that whatever happened they must keep the line to Batt. H.Q. clear I went to sleep.

During that day it rained, making the 'going' more impossible than ever. Before dusk I had a message through over the wire cancelling the order to attack.

From my description of this part of the line I think it must have been Nieuport (*Nieuwpoort*).

August 28th. Leave front line 5 a.m. Arrive Oost
Dunkerke (*Oostduinkerke*) 8 a.m. Leave Oost Dunkerke
10 a.m. Arrive La Panne (*De Panne*) 12 noon.

I see that there is no entry for August 27th. I suppose I plodded round my part of the line during the night, but my only recollection of it is the 'post', the canal, and the river, and mud as far as the eye could see.

When we left the line at 5 a.m. on the 28th it was drizzling with rain and very dark. After their sojourn in the mud all the men were somewhat exhausted and it was a very dreary march from 5 to 8 a.m.; a large part of the way the road was cobbles and very slippery. The Battalion had to march out by platoons on account of the first part of the road being shelled; we were wet, muddy, cold, and tired and no doubt looked a very sorry crew. We went so slowly and took so long that at one time I was afraid that we had missed our way. When we arrived at Oost Dunkerke I thought that at last we were at our destination. After the officers had been round to see that all the men were in and had somewhere to lie down (they were too weary to eat), we also lay down in our billet. No sooner were we asleep than I got orders that we were to start again at once.

There was much cursing and swearing and it was only with considerable difficulty that we got the company paraded and ready to march off. We had, I think, been the last company to come in. We then had to march a further four miles or so to La Panne where we arrived at noon, dead beat.

August 29th. Leave La Panne for near Synthe. Arrive 12 noon.

Here we evidently had a good night's rest.

August 30th. Inspection of clothing etc.

Extract from letter dated August 30th:

'Had a lot of new and quite novel experiences this time up the line. Being shelled by a 15-inch armour-piercing delayed-action howitzer shell, which when it went off shook the whole place just like my old friend the mine going up. Having to cross a river on a three foot wooden bridge on floats that the Huns delighted in shelling. A taste of the new mustard gas which now no one thinks much of. A damn funny bit of the line one way and

A British 15-inch howitzer.

another. Having once seen it I was not sorry to leave it. Another officer that had been a long time with the Batt. killed.'

August 31st. Leave for Moulle near St. Omar (*St Omer*). Arrive 2.30 p.m.

September 6th. Go to training ground, meet Duncan.

Duncan is brother-in-law.

September 7th. Ride with McLennan.

September 8th. Dine with Duncan at Watten.

Duncan was in the A.S.C. It was very interesting to me to see in what luxury the A.S.C. lived compared with the Infantry. A bed, clean sheets and blankets, etc. Bath and wash-basin and a small room in a hut to themselves. I heard one of them complain bitterly that at one time he was unable to keep his hut warm even with the fire going all night!! Even then he said the water in his wash-basin had been frozen. Ye gods! A fire and bed, and a wash-basin and then to complain of the cold.

September 9th. On Court Martial. President Maj. Poore, other member Templar 20th R.F.

September 10th. Fire on range. Duncan dines with C Coy.

September 11th. Route March. Forty-two men on 30 yard range.

September 12th. To 'A' Training Ground.

September 13th. Shooting 'B' Range.

September 15th. Leave Moulle 10 a.m. Arrive
   Lederzelle (*Lederzeele*).

September 16th. Leave Lederzelle. Arrive some place.

September 17th. Leave some place. Arrive Caestre
   8 a.m.

September 18th. Smith returns.

September 21st. Meet Will. In camp M8a3.2.

M8a3.2. is a map reference.

September 24th. Leave tents. Go to reserve line Ypres.
   Occupy trenches near Stirling Castle.

It was said that every soldier, if he lived, eventually came
to the Ypres salient for his sins. The Battalion had not
been in the salient since 1914 and there were few if any
still with the Battalion that had been in Ypres before.
Although we did not like the place we were all rather
interested to be there after having heard so much about
it during the last two years. I felt quite bucked at going
there. Nearly the whole of the salient was under Boche

observation. During the day we were in the reserve line just by the banks of the canal. We got a certain amount of shelling but nothing very bad. I am not sure but think we were by the ramparts.

I had orders at dusk to take my company up and occupy a position at Stirling Castle, a well known place but nothing to see there except shallow, very muddy and wet trenches. The whole place was more or less under water. I had great difficulty in finding the place, largely because I thought there would be something by which to recognise it and there was in fact nothing. After squelching round in the mud for a long time I stumbled on a company of machine gunners, who told me that that spot was Stirling Castle. We then proceeded to take up our position as well as we could; there was no trench to speak of but plenty of water.

Rather against my wiser instincts I took as Company H.Q. an old Pill Box that had had a direct hit on it and had been half knocked over. It was not a good place to occupy as it might be used by the Boche as a mark to fire at. I took it because it was the only spot that could be distinguished in the sea of mud and an easy one to which to find my way back and for 'runners' to return to. It was a hopeless place to sit or be in as it was leaning at an angle, difficult to get into, and was one or more feet deep in water. It smelt very bad and I suspected dead bodies under it somewhere.

A Pill Box is a room built on the ground about 7 feet by 7 inside and made of very thick concrete with two or three loop holes; the entrance is very low down and small, on the opposite side to the enemy. A direct hit from a big gun might kill the occupants but would not smash up the Pill Box.

The following morning as soon as it was light I tried by taking bearings with my compass to find my exact position on the map. It was very important to know exactly where I was, as otherwise I would only roughly guess my way to other positions. There had been a bit of fighting during the last few days and no one was quite sure of the positions of our front line or advanced posts. Owing to the difficulty of finding any landmarks on the sea of mud, compass bearings were not very informative. I believe that I eventually got my position fairly accurately from the machine gun company officer and was then able to check it. The machine gunners were firing on 'night lines' and in consequence had to know the exact position on the map of each gun.

Firing on a 'night line' meant that they fired on a certain compass bearing, generally at night. The trajectory was high and well above any of our lines, the guns were laid at a certain angle so that the bullets landed on ground that the Boche might be using at night, or would use if they were making an attack. In other words the machine guns were used on the same principle as the field guns. The machine guns in question were firing off and on all night. The shelling was very general but not unduly heavy.

I found that Stirling Castle was more or less a support line and some hundreds of yards from the positions our advanced posts or front line was suspected to occupy.

That night of the 24th was mostly spent in getting the company out into some sort of orderly position, getting rid of some of the mud and attempting to clean the place up a bit. We were always supposed to try and leave every position we occupied better than we found it and unless it was badly shelled generally did do so. It was not much good trying to rest in the Pill Box on account of there being so much water and stink in it.

September 25th. In same place. Big attack at 5.50 a.m. Boche counter attacks.

I knew that the attack was coming off as I had had orders to stand by for it, with rifles clear of coverings and magazines charged. If our attack was successful I expected to have to follow it up, or if the Boche counter attacked I might have to counter counter-attack. Anyhow at 5.50 a.m. our shelling started and thousands of shells came whistling over our position and we could see them exploding on the German lines. Our barrage was as heavy as any I had seen and the noise was terrific. Very soon the Boche started to return the compliment but most of

No man's land at night.

their shells were landing between us and the front line. However, they started to shell the machine gun company that was just by us, every gun of which company was blazing away as fast as it could and some of these shells landed amongst us. The machine gunners suffered rather badly and had several guns with their teams knocked out. Very soon after it was light messages started coming through to me enquiring how the attack was, what casualties I was getting and had any one come back from the front line.

I watched the front line through my field glasses from the top of a little hillock and sometimes thought I saw

249

our men and sometimes the Boche, but was never very certain as they all more or less looked like animated lumps of mud. A few wounded men started to dribble back, some of whom said the attack was a great success and some that it was a 'bloody washout'.

I sent back what reports I could but knew that they were of no value. As the day progressed the messages I received became more urgent in demanding news and it was evident that H.Q. had little idea how the attack was going. Neither had I, scouts I sent out failed to return, wounded men all gave different versions, and through my field glasses I could make out nothing. All this time we were 'standing to' ready to move off at a moment's notice. As night approached and it became dark the chaotic conditions grew worse. Very lights were going up all over the place, aeroplanes were dropping star shells and the shelling from each side became worse. One message after another continued to arrive. Had I still got both my officers? How many men had I still got? Were the Boche putting a barrage on such and such a place? Get ready to move. On no account leave your position; and so on.

The German shelling became more intense as it grew darker, and then all of a sudden they started shelling like blazes and I knew something was going to happen. After a few minutes an S.O.S. rocket went up from our front line and Very light after Very light followed. And then all along our front S.O.S. after S.O.S. went shooting up into the sky; I remarked that the attack had developed into a Brock's benefit display. The Boche were counter attacking in force all down the line. By this time all our guns had commenced drum fire on their counter attack lines, what machine guns were left near us recommenced continuous rapid fire on their counter attack night lines and pandemonium reigned. The whole country was bright with gun flashes, shell explosions, rifle fire, rockets and Very lights; the noise was of course deafening. Then I got a message through by an exhausted runner telling me to immediately send an officer to go as fast as he could with twenty men to the front line to attach himself to a certain Battalion that had evidently had very heavy casualties and was in a bad way. I only had two officers and one had only been a short time with the Company. One was I think Smith, the other's name I do not remember. I sent the latter with the whole of his platoon of only about 20 men. He was a stout-hearted fellow and went off in very good form.

I could not tell him exactly where he had to go to but told him he must report to the Battalion I told him and no other, not to stop till he got there and to hurry. I attempted to impress on him as deeply as I could that he must go to the Battalion he was told to go to and not to get drawn into any other fights or seduced into reinforcing any other Battalion that wanted help, as if he did not get to the right place I should get Hell and all the blame. He

Traffic on the Menin Road.

was a jovial, humorous chap with a thin face, I did not expect to see him again and was sorry to lose him. I felt sure we should have some dirty work to do before the night was over.

September 26th. At night am ordered to take up
    position on Menin Road. Wigan makes mistake.

All that night of the 25th–26th the strafe continued, the song of the shells rising and falling in bursts, but continuing all the time. More wounded came filtering back but now they all told the same story, they said it was Hell up in front, that the Boche were counter attacking in great numbers and in many places had broken through and that the casualties were very heavy indeed on both sides. We were all very much on the qui vive expecting the blighters to come down on us any moment, particularly as they were now shelling behind us, and no longer our position at Stirling Castle. I began to regret having lost one officer and platoon. Then I got a message telling me that the Boche were reported to be attacking in great force down the Menin Road and to be prepared to move at a moment's notice. I was not in the least surprised as I had for some time been expecting something of the sort.

Then I got a message through from the platoon I had sent up to the front line. They had found the Battalion and the officer had reported to the C.O. They had then been sent to reinforce one of the companies, shortly afterwards a shell had landed amongst them and the officer was badly wounded. This was the last I heard from them.

The next message I got was from my Batt. H.Q. which told me that I was to take over command of 'D' Coy. and with my own Coy. and 'D' Coy. go to a certain map reference where I should find some old unoccupied trenches. That I was to occupy these trenches and hold them to repel the German attack that was being pushed down the Menin Road. To acknowledge the message and then move off with all speed and report when I was in position.

The map reference given was a spot about 100 yards on the left of the Menin Road with a swamp on its left front. I told my only officer, Smith I think it was, to get the Company ready to move off and to explain to the N.C.O.s where we had to go to and what we had to do. I then floundered off in the dark to find 'D' Coy.

A young regular officer new to the Battalion, called Wigan, was in command. He with the shelling, the darkness, and the chaotic conditions was in a rather confused state. I explained to him where he had to go to and sent him off at once with some of his Company, telling him to send back guides immediately he got there and that I would meet these guides as I was following him immediately. I then sent back a message acknowledging the message I had received and confirming the map reference. Having done which I started off with a few men, the remainder of the two companies following me. I met no guides and could not see Wigan anywhere. I knew that if I mucked things up and got half the Battalion stranded in the wrong place I should never hear the end of it and I was becoming bewildered and nervous. I halted all the platoons that were following me, sent off men to try and find Wigan and went scouting round myself.

We were still on the wrong side of the road but facing the way we should go. What I should have done was to have taken all the men with me to the right position and then sent off to find those that were with Wigan. But it was very dark, we had come in a great hurry, and might have lost direction and I was not *certain* where I was. Wigan had had more time and he *might* be in the right place whilst I was going wrong. The fact that the matter was so urgent and important added to my confusion. Then some man loomed out of the darkness and said that Wigan and the men with him were on our right.

I then felt certain he was in the wrong place because we had not crossed the road; however, I decided that as time was passing and the Boche might be advancing we had better be altogether and prepared than unprepared, on the move and scattered. So we turned off to our right and went up to the position Wigan had taken up. The two companies were put out on an extended line facing obliquely the Menin Road and began digging themselves in as hard as they could. The position tactically appeared sound but it was the wrong one and I had no idea what was on our front or our flanks.

Poor old Wigan was in a state of shock. I was very annoyed and abusive but could get little out of him; he acknowledged the position was the wrong one but said he had done his best. He annoyed me intensely by time and again coming up to me and asking me if he was killed to tell everyone and write home to his people saying he had done his best and died fighting. I stuck it for some time as the poor chap was suffering very much but I had quite enough trouble without him and eventually shut him up.

By this time the Boche were putting a heavy barrage on the road where we should cross it and also, as far as I could see, on the position that we should have been occupying. I sent back a message to H.Q. giving them my exact position etc., and saying that the road and the position to which we were ordered was being heavily shelled. I naturally got a message back that was far from polite and telling me to go to where I was told and quickly. This we proceeded to do; but for an hour the men had been hard at work digging themselves in and were highly disgusted at all their labour being wasted. Fortunately, as we moved off in one long line, the shelling eased off and we crossed the road and skirted the swamp without I think any casualties.

I found the old trenches that were our correct position without any trouble and the two companies proceeded to occupy them. The men were very exhausted, and except for the few that had to go on sentry duty, all of them lay down in the mud and went to sleep. I still feared the expected attack and could not sleep and as I wandered round I marvelled at the way the men slept on even when occasional shells came over and exploded near them.

Dawn came and no Boche attack had reached us; now that we were in the right position I did not know whether to be sorry or glad. We could have given a very good account of ourselves as we commanded at least 800 yards of the road over and along which they would have had to come and on our left front was a swamp that would have caused them to bunch together on the road and be an easy mark. With the light I could see where we had wandered during the night and the place where we had wrongly 'dug in'.

September 27th. Leave position on Menin Road; return to Stirling Castle.

Soon after it was light a message came through telling me to take the two companies back to Stirling Castle. As we started a few shells came over and near us. It may be that we were seen by Boche observers, or it may have been the usual shelling of the road. Anyhow a few men were hit and the stretcher-bearers were called up, the rest of the two companies hurrying on. Then the stretcher-bearers went on and I followed. When they were well past the road in a (fortunately) very muddy part a shell landed right amongst them, and they all appeared to be knocked over; I went on expecting to find most of them killed or wounded but to my surprise they all picked themselves up and went on apparently unhurt, but one of the wounded men had again been hit. We got back to Stirling Castle without any further trouble and stayed there for the rest of that day.

September 28th. Am wounded about 11 a.m. whilst coming out of the line. To Aid post A.D.S. C.C.S.

During the night of the 27th–28th we received orders to rendezvous at some place back behind the line. The ground we would have to cover was being intermittently shelled and I sent the Company off by sections with intervals of about 30 yards; this took very much longer but was safer. For the first two miles they had to go over ground that was entirely shell pitted. By this I mean that the lip of one shell-hole was also the lip of the next one with no level ground anywhere. Over a portion of this ground duck boards had been laid; these not only served to make the going easier but also to indicate the right direction. There were of course a good many blank places where the duck boards had been blown away by shells. The shell-holes were full of water and the mud ankle deep. Progress was slow. There was one great disadvantage these duck boards had and that was that they attracted shell fire. I gave the last section to leave a good start, as they would move slower than I, and then started off with my servant McLennan and McDougal the Coy. H.Q. cook.

McDougal who I have not mentioned before deserves a paragraph to himself. He was a man rather older than the general run, and a quiet, well-spoken chap. It was partly for these reasons that he had been made cook for the officers' mess, he knew nothing about cooking, and could not rise above cold bully beef turned out of a tin. Whenever I asked him what he was going to give us to eat he replied: 'How would you like some nice cold beef?' I, knowing what he meant, always replied: 'Not at all.' But he always gave it to us. He was a very nice chap, had a wife and family in Glasgow, and was quite well educated. He was also very deaf, and did not hear a lot that was said to him. I think that the shelling had made his hearing worse. For all the above reasons I had managed fairly often to leave him behind when we went up to the front line. There was an arrangement by which about six men could be left behind every time we went up. This was the first occasion I had taken him to the trenches for some time. There was no unfairness in leaving him behind more often than the others as all agreed that he was unsuited for the more violent form of warfare. Having a liking for those who are deaf I used to laugh and joke with him a lot in a loud voice and whenever I pulled his leg he used to give a very cheerful sheepish grin. Nothing was ever too much trouble for him and although far from strong he always did his very best.

Well he, McLennan and I started off I suppose about 3.30 a.m. and as few other people were about in daylight we got along fairly quickly. A few shells were coming over but not many, also they were landing in the mud and were in consequence not very dangerous.

Dawn over Passchendaele, autumn 1917.

When we were about 100 yards from a road where the
duck boards ended I, who was leading, stopped rather
ostentatiously, to show my contempt for the shells, and
knocking out my pipe proceeded to light a cigarette. I
passed some joke to the other two who I could see were
anxious to get on and out of it all. All this time solitary
shells were landing on different parts of the road along
which we had to go to the right. It was that part of our

journey that I least relished. We got on to the road and started off at a quicker pace; McLennan on my right and McDougal a little behind me on my left. Before we had gone fifty yards a shell came over and landed about ten yards behind us. Either the noise or the concussion made me spin round and a small bit of the shell casing cut through the left side of my collar just by the front stud and then through my throat where it came up flop against my wind pipe.

'Are you hit?' said McLennan.

'Yes', I replied, 'got it in the neck', this incidentally being a pun as the statement besides being true was a common expression of the time meaning to be severely hit either physically or morally.

We saw poor old McDougal lying dead or dying. I was not feeling very bright myself and although I was not bleeding much externally expected that I was bleeding a lot internally as I felt rather choky and wanted to cough. McLennan was untouched and whilst I retired to a shell-hole at the side of the road he attended to poor McDougal.

In a few seconds he came back, said McDougal was dead, and wanted to put a field dressing on my wound. This I told him was unnecessary as I was not bleeding to any extent. I then started to cough and brought up some blood and the bit of shell which must have stuck in my wind pipe. McLennan very kindly retrieved the bit of iron out of the mud and handing it to me remarked that I might like it to keep. This I did and my wife has it now.

PATCHING UP THE "PIPPED"   *Canadian Official.*

In a few moments as I felt quite fit and did not think I was going to die just yet we started off again, hoping to come to an ambulance station. I then discovered that my voice was going, which somewhat distressed me, and also McLennan who thought I was dying as I walked.

He was very concerned and kept on asking me if I could keep on. This made me wonder if I could, and I began to think I was much worse than I was. As a matter of fact there was very little the matter with me except that I was blowing bubbles through the hole in my neck and could only just talk in a very weak whisper. Then in the distance we saw an Advanced Dressing Station which I believe was one of the first American ones, anyhow there was an American doctor there.

There were several other wounded men waiting to be attended to, so I said goodbye to McLennan and sat down. When my turn came the doctor put a large dressing on the wound and then pumped some anti-tetanus serum into the skin on my chest, put me on a stretcher and told me not to move. I immediately went to sleep.

The next thing that I remember is being in a bed with clean sheets in a Casualty Clearing Station and being told to lie still. I felt very much alive and interested in myself but the air going in and out of the hole in my neck annoyed me. I was also interested in a man in the bed opposite me who would keep on getting out or trying to do so, he was delirious and was talking to

FIRST LINE HOSPITAL.   *Canadian Official.*

himself all the time, then he died and they took him away on a stretcher.

Shortly afterwards much to my surprise my brother Will came in to see me, he bucked me up a lot by telling me that bar complications, which were unlikely, I would be quite alright, and that the wound would soon heal up, and my voice which had completely gone would in due course return to me. He told me that McLennan had got back to the Battalion and had told them of McDougal being killed and said that I was very seriously wounded and that he did not expect me to live. I had been reported killed several times before but this time I expect they thought it was true.

My next recollection is of lying on a stretcher on a

264

railway siding waiting for a train to come in and then being lifted up and very gently slipped on to a top bunk in a hospital train, and then again being told that I must on no account move.

September 29th. Arrive D. of W. Hospital 9 a.m.

This, the Duchess of Westminster's Hospital, was at Le Touquet or Paris Plage, the place where I had been for 4 days' leave a few months before. The Old Casino had been laid out in wards.

The hospital was quite full. I was taken from the train in a motor ambulance that I noticed was driven by a rather nice-looking girl, carried into the hospital and gently slipped into a bed and once again told I must on no account move. I have never quite understood the reason for this constant repetition of being told on no account to move; but suppose the wound must have been very close to one of the arteries in the neck, and that the doctors, fearing the artery might break through, had put something to that effect on the label that was tied on to me. I had certainly not been allowed anything to eat or drink since I was wounded and was allowed to swallow nothing for another day or two. Strangely enough I suffered no inconvenience from this enforced abstinence.

This hospital was well run and I was very well looked after. It was very full and had many bad cases.

September 30th. In D. of W. Hospital.

October 1st. In same place.

Extract from letter dated October 1st:

'Am getting on very well. At present the hole in my neck is plugged up, soon after the plug is pulled I hope to return to England. This is a nice hospital but I think I should be much better if they would allow me to get up and did not starve me . . . My wound gives me little or no pain . . . Cannot smoke now. Curse it.'

October 2nd. Same place. Leave Hospital 11 p.m.

In the afternoon I was told I was being sent home that night. About an hour before I was taken off my bed, a nurse came and gave me an injection, morphia I think, and the next thing I remember was being put in a train at some English sea port.

October 3rd. Arrive A.W.H. for officers 7 p.m.

In the train my bandages got loose and the wound a bit dirty which gave trouble but not much to me. When we arrived at Charing Cross we were taken off in motor ambulances; as each ambulance left the station a big crowd

H. E. Camidge, J. O. Davies, F. O. Crawford, H. Burchell, A. R. Cope, E. Cooke, W. G. Collins, J. E. Coutts,
C.S.M. Broadley, I. G. Davies, L. G. Arnold, W. F. Benson, T. R. Boorman, R. Bolley, J. H. Conroy, H. M. Crowther, R. W. Blundell, S. Bell, W. P. Cutbush,
G. A. Cotton, L. G. Coxhead, L. A. Corner, A. Craig, Capt. A. J. Stewart, m.c., W. Davies, A. G. Currington, F. Cross, E. W. Bone.

20th Officers' Cadet Battalion 1918, with my grandfather
in the middle of the front row.

shouted out 'Good luck' etc. I was taken to the American
Womens' Hospital for Officers in Lancaster Gate.

I could not have gone to a better hospital nor have been
better treated than I was there. Nor could I have chosen a
position that better suited me or was more convenient. My
future wife lived just the other side of the park.

My War Diary so far as my own particular war was
concerned may be said here to end. On October 6th I
was allowed to have a bath. On November 6th I with

many thanks and regrets on my part left the American Women's Hospital, as I had been ordered to a convalescent hospital at 19 Hyde Park Gardens and there I stayed for a few more weeks.

On December 27th I was married and on December 31st I went to the 20th Officers Cadet Battalion to which Battalion I had been ordered as an instructor on light duty. Here I remained till the beginning of 1919, at which time had the war continued I was due to return to France.

Epilogue

Although for my grandfather the war was now over, the fighting, of course, continued. The Third Battle of Ypres ended with the Canadian capture of Passchendaele in November 1917; 53,000 British troops had been killed, with another 200,000 wounded. By then the Bolsheviks had seized power in Russia and were suing for peace on any terms. The Italian army had been crushed at the Battle of Caporetto. These two events enabled the Germans to concentrate their forces in France, and in March 1918 they unleashed a series of massive offensives. The Allied armies gave up much of the ground they had so painfully won in the previous two years and buckled. They did not break, though, while the German army was now exhausted. In July and August, the Allies, reinforced by ever greater numbers of American soldiers, retook the initiative and began raining down a series of hammer blows, all along the line, which drove back and shattered the German army. At the same time, Germany's allies were collapsing.

The return of the Children

9 October 1917, a postcard from his niece: *'Dear Uncle, very many happy returns of tomorrow. I hope you will soon be better.'*

Domestic morale, sapped by food shortages caused by naval blockade, crumbled. On 11 November 1918, the Germans effectively surrendered, and my grandfather, together with millions of others, was spared a return to the front.

In keeping with the fashion for reticence of his generation, the finer details of what happened to Captain Alexander Julian Hartley ('Tim') Stewart after the end of the Great War are not particularly apparent. Although my father, Thomas Howard Stewart, was close to him, as is evidenced by the joint fishing holidays and the fact that I have such vivid memories of the flat in Eastbourne, it was not my grandfather's habit to do anything like confide in his younger son. Relations between fathers and sons were not as intimate then as they often are now.

It appears, however, that after the war he married Margarita Cameron Macdonald and moved to Carlton Gardens in Putney, where his first son, William, was born in 1919, and his second, Thomas, in 1923. The family then moved to a maisonette in Linden Gardens, Notting Hill, for ten years. He and his brother ran their own business as tea and rubber brokers in the City, and in 1936 he moved to a large block of flats in Olympia just after also buying a cottage in Long Wittenham, in Oxfordshire; he divided his time between the two homes.

Though eager to serve on the outbreak of the Second World War, he was deemed too old to rejoin his old regiment, the Cameronians, so he first became an ARP warden, during the Battle of Britain in September 1940, and then joined the Royal Artillery and went up to Prestwick, Glasgow, where he operated as Anti-Aircraft Liaison Officer on the airfield. After the war he went back to London and his work, living in a private hotel in Notting Hill, along the Bayswater Road, during the week and returning to Long Wittenham at the weekends. In the 1950s he and his wife sold the cottage and bought a flat in Eastbourne, where his wife lived full time and which he inhabited at the weekends after his work in London. He died of leukaemia in 1965 at the age of eighty-three, having continued to work up to the very last.

The Historical Relevance
of Captain Stewart's Diary

TO MANY people nowadays, the most famous British officer of the Great War is the fictional television character Captain Edmund Blackadder. The 1989 comedy series *Blackadder Goes Forth* in many ways summarises the popular perception of that conflict. 'The mud, the blood, the *endless* poetry'. General Haig casually sweeps toy soldiers off the battlefield as one mindless offensive after another is launched to move his cocktail cabinet six inches closer to Berlin. Wine-faced generals, safe in their châteaux, demand unthinking obedience of soldiers who plod through the mud of no man's land into the teeth of German machine guns and are cut down in swathes.

The picture of the British army that emerges from my grandfather's diary in some ways confirms this image. For instance, there is little evidence that he was ever told the reason for what he was asked to do. We sense his growing frustration at generals who order attacks without fully understanding the situation on the ground. His resentment towards the 'gilded staff', and his perception of the divide that existed between the full-time regular officers and the 'temporary gentlemen' like himself, are themes that come through strongly in many other First World War memoirs and diaries. The same goes for ever-present companions such as lice, rats, cold, disease and, of course, death.

Much of this, of course, was not new to the First World War. Junior officers and soldiers throughout history have rarely been privy to their masters' grand strategic designs. Ill feeling between the fighting men and what Shakespeare lampooned as the 'popinjay' staff officer, 'fresh as a bridegroom' and 'perfumèd like a milliner' in *Henry IV Part I*, is as old as war. Fighting has always been a sordid affair. In 1914–18, true, the population was exposed to the squalor of war on a previously unknown scale. But life at this time, in an inner-city tenement or peasant's cottage, was frequently itself 'nasty, brutish and short'.

In other ways, the diary undercuts the popular image. Unthinking obedience was not universally demanded. My grandfather mentions how Colonel Chaplin had managed to have a futile assault cancelled in 1915. Robert Graves documents another such case involving Chaplin in February 1917; and my grandfather himself succeeds in stopping a third.

The battles he describes do not fit our stereotype at all. My grandfather fought in the three great British battles of 1916–17: the Somme, Arras and Third Ypres. At High

Wood on 20 July 1916, rather than using the long slow-moving infantry lines of myth, the attack is tactically complex, professionally executed and succeeds in its objectives, albeit at such high cost that the position is untenable. At Arras, in May the next year, they try an innovative early afternoon attack but are unable to consolidate early success. Finally, the Australian attack on Polygon Wood in September 1917, which the Cameronians support, takes place over dry, indeed dusty, ground, rather than the mud for which Passchendaele is notorious. It is completely successful.

Further, the ethos of paternalism which suffused the British army comes through strongly in the diary. The policy of rotating units for rest; home leave; the emphasis placed on the maintenance of morale through frequent mail and reliable rations; the inspection of men's feet; the 'team-building' exercises of boxing, football, horse shows and concert parties – all testify to an attempt, within the limits of contemporary attitudes, to maximise the welfare of the men. Battle casualties aside, many soldiers enjoyed better health in the army than they had at home, and put on weight. Contemporaries certainly considered the British record in this regard, compared with the French or German, exemplary.

My grandfather's diary was written under stress, and revisited more than ten years later. Inevitably, and quite understandably, some inaccuracies crept in. The story he tells on 26 May 1916, for example, of a labour battalion helping to retake Red Dragon Crater, is true, but actually took place on 22 June. Likewise, he conflates the German attack of 25 September 1917 with the Allied assault on Polygon Wood the next day.

Such quibbles miss the point, however, that a more interesting way to look at the diary is in terms of his overall experience of the First World War. How representative was it? How did the war change him?

In the play and film *Oh! What a Lovely War* we see innocent young men flocking to the colours on the outbreak of war, swept along by patriotism, expecting it all to be over by Christmas, only to have their naive illusions shattered in the mud as the aristocratic 'donkeys' who lead them betray their trust and send them to futile deaths. This potent strand of the Great War myth is an invention. The greatest influx of volunteers occurred *after* the scale of losses had become known, and 100,000 men a month were still joining up at the end of 1915. Certainly, on the evidence of this diary, my grandfather was never such a victim. When he joined up, he was thirty-three years old, and knew, as well as anyone could – the casualty figures were not kept secret – the risks involved. He was, though, determined to do his duty. As he did.

And yet, as the war drags on, his fatalism grows. He can feel the odds shifting against him. His health breaks down more frequently. His need for leave grows increasingly desperate. He mentions going to church more. He makes no secret of the fact that he finds it ever harder to subvert his fear. Lord Moran, a doctor on the Western Front, and later Churchill's physician in the Second World War, used a striking metaphor for the draining away of courage:

> Courage is will-power, whereof no man has an unlimited stock; and when in war it is used up, he is finished. A man's courage is his capital and he is always spending. The call on the bank may be only the daily drain of the front line or it may be a sudden draft which threatens to close the account. His will is perhaps almost destroyed by intensive shelling, by heavy bombing, or by a bloody battle, or it is gradually used up by monotony, by exposure, by the loss of stauncher spirits on whom he has come to depend, by physical exhaustion, by a wrong attitude to danger, to casualties, to war, to death itself.

My grandfather, like many of his generation, but thankfully not ours, had to face this process. He never went 'bankrupt'. He learnt to relax and take pleasure where he could. We get no sense he gloried in the war. His job was distasteful, but he thought it necessary, and saw it through as best he was able. When war came to Europe again in 1939, he was prepared once more to serve.

We find it hard today to understand the fortitude of men like him in such conditions. We think any war insane, and the First World War especially so. We see such men through the prism of ninety years of literature, film and poetry. We tend to impute modern attitudes and responses to our grandfathers and great-grandfathers. Because they are only a couple of generations away, we sometimes forget how different their mentality could be. To try to see them as they would have seen themselves requires more effort on our part. But it is, perhaps, the best tribute we can pay their memory.

Some Notes on Leave, Family and Social Life

NO TV, no radio, and movies and recorded music in their infancy – compared to our own era, in which almost every activity is frequently accompanied by recorded music, and in which access to a vast choice of entertainment media is but a button-press away, the First World War seems almost to have been life without a soundtrack.

And yet it wasn't. This generation had a wealth of entertainment options. The difference was just that entertainment was a live, communal experience involving input and interaction on the part of the audience. Relaxing on the sofa in front of a video was not yet even imagined. Instead, one had to go out and mingle with other people, at the theatre, the music hall, in a restaurant, or eating with friends and family in one another's homes. In many ways, this generation must have been far more socially aware and accomplished than we are today. Judging by my grandfather's movements while on leave, and even when he was behind the lines in France, they were certainly extremely socially active.

Of course, the fact that they were living through the bloodiest war in history and no fighting man had any great expectations of surviving far beyond the end of his leave must have contributed hugely to the desire for a full social agenda, wherever the opportunity presented itself. My grandfather's comment about 17 April 1917, '. . . another leave over. I could hardly expect to come back again unless sent home wounded', is eclipsed only by the poignant image of the 'pitiable sight' of the women on the platform as the train departs after his earlier break. 'Eat, drink and be merry for tomorrow we may die' can scarcely ever have seemed a more appropriate philosophy.

Even so, my grandfather's social life while on leave does appear to have been particularly energetic. When he claims to have been spending most of his time in bed with fever and rheumatism (in fact probably due to one of the recurrent attacks of malaria which he contracted before the war in Malay and which plagued him for many years), he still manages to go out every night for dinner, the theatre or both. In the interests of giving a fully rounded picture of the man and his life, and finding points of reference with which we can identify today, where were these places he went on leave, what were the shows he went to see, and who were the people he dined with?

The first leave he mentions is only five days long, just

after his thirty-fourth birthday on 9 October 1916. Three days prior to this, he has been immersed in carrying out practice attacks and 11-mile training marches; this is also the first leave he has had since he departed for the front in the third week of March. When one considers what he has lived through in the interim, one can imagine that the temporary shift back into civilised society must have been extraordinarily bewildering. He arrives in London at 4 p.m., has a Turkish bath at the RAC and then travels down to Richmond (Pyrland Cottage) to stay with his brother Tommy and his wife, Jessica. The stop-off at the Royal Automobile Club (then, as now, situated at 89/91 Pall Mall) was not untypical of other officers home on leave. The building had opened for business in March 1911; during the First World War it became effectively an officers' club, part of which was used by the British Red Cross Society, and by September 1918 it had provided 'bed, breakfast and baths for 228,125 officers and served approximately 2,000,000 meals'.[1]

Thence, after this very brief transitional wash-and-brush-up, to Tommy, Jessica and 'normal' life in Richmond. Of the three brothers, Alexander (known as 'Tim' ever since some aunt had exclaimed, 'Ooh, what a tiny Tim!' on seeing him as a baby in his cot) was the youngest, Tommy next and Will the eldest. It was Tommy, a tea trader (who for unknown reasons did not go to the war), with whom my grandfather ran a rubber and tea broker's under the name of Charles Hope and Sons, from offices on the top floor of Plantation House, in Fenchurch Street, for the rest of their civilian lives. Plantation House has long been one of the best-known buildings in the City of London; it still stands, having undergone substantial renovation in 1991. Jessica, Tommy's wife, I knew myself, though for some reason she was always referred to as Trixie. She had been married before she wed Tommy, to a man called Moseley, who had drowned when the *Lusitania* was sunk on 7 May 1915, so her marriage to Tommy must have been fairly recent at this point. My memories are of a charming old lady who insisted on having cheese and biscuits between the main course and pudding, and who never wrote directly on Christmas or birthday cards, always preferring to insert a little piece of loose card with a greeting on it. The idea, thoughtful if a little eccentric, was that the recipient would then be able to use the card again.

'Guv' or 'The Gov'nor', whom my grandfather sees on 13 October, refers to his father William, a doctor; 'Uncle' is most probably his uncle by marriage, the Col. (Alfred) Delavoye who assisted my grandfather's application to the Cameronians. William did have a brother, Charles, but Charles's decision to marry the daughter of a butcher had earlier caused William to disown him for twenty years.

The Empire is now the Empire Cinema in Leicester Square, combined with the Club Equinox next door – it became separated from the cinema, as the Empire Ballroom, in 1967. At the time the two brothers visited before dining out in Piccadilly, it was predominantly a music hall staging variety shows, although it is possible they saw a 'moving picture' show there – in 1896 the Empire was reputedly the first venue in Britain to show a commercial projected film, by the Lumière Brothers, and in 1916 it was running programmes that included live performances and short film shows.[2]

On 14 October my grandfather 'Dine(s) Stillmans' with Will and Laure. Stillmans appears not to be a restaurant, but very probably the surname of the husband of Maudie, Col. Delavoye's daughter, and thus Tim's cousin, with whom he dines again later in the week. Laure was Will's wife, and a Belgian.

It was Will, another doctor, who broke the good news to my grandfather that he would likely make a full recovery from his wounds. The essential and uncanny piece of the story missing from the diary, but handed down through the family, is that apparently my wounded grandfather had initially been set aside as one of those 'unlikely to make it'. It was a fortunate coincidence that Will happened to be passing through that area of the line at the time, stumbled across his brother, recognised that his wounds were not as life-threatening as they had first seemed, and rescued him from being left to die.

Potash and Perlmutter, which my grandfather takes my grandmother to see before treating her to tea at the Savoy, was a hit comedy by Montague Glass and Charles Klein, based on a series of stories by Glass about a pair of Jewish American tailors. It had rave reviews when it opened in New York and was brought to the Queen's Theatre, Shaftesbury Avenue (currently, in 2008, home to *Les Misérables*), by the producers Edward Laurillard and George Grossmith Jr, for a long run, in 1914. It spawned a series of films, commencing in 1923.[3]

My grandfather's other specific theatrical outings are to the Gaiety Theatre, and to see *High Jinks* and *Chu Chin Chow*. The Gaiety was a West End theatre situated at the intersection of the Aldwych and the Strand. It had started life as the Strand Music Hall in the 1860s, and at the time of Tim and Rita's visit it specialised in musical comedy. The show they went to see would have been *Theodore and Co.*, produced by Sir Alfred Butt and Austin Hurgon and written by Grossmith Jr, with music by Ivor Novello and Jerome Kern. It starred Leslie Henson (father of today's Nicky Henson) and Fred Leslie, opened at the Gaiety on 19 September 1916 and ran for 500 performances. The theatre itself closed in 1939 and never reopened after sustaining bomb damage in the Second World War.[4] The site is now the location for a new hotel designed by Sir Norman Foster. It is interesting to note that my grandfather and Rita went to the Gaiety again, on 28 March 1917, on his next leave, when *Theodore and Co.* must still have been running. According to my father, Tim was distinctly

unmusical, so presumably Rita had a fondness for this
particular show.

High Jinks, which they see on 17 October, the night
before his first return to the front, was a reworking of a
Rudolf Friml show, written by Frederick Lonsdale (grandfather of Edward and James Fox; great-grandfather of
Emilia Fox), with music by Howard Talbot, Kern and
Paul Rubens, and showing at the Royal Adelphi Theatre
in the Strand, now called simply the Adelphi Theatre, and
in 2008 hosting the current production of *Joseph and His
Amazing Technicolor Dreamcoat*.[5] *Chu Chin Chow*, the only
other show mentioned by name, was based on the Arabian
Nights story of *Ali Baba and the Forty Thieves*. It cost over
£5,000 to produce, at His Majesty's Theatre, Haymarket
(now Her Majesty's, and home to *Phantom of the Opera*),
and, at 2,238 performances, became the longest-running
musical, prior to *Salad Days* in the mid-1950s.[6]

Clearly, my grandfather did all he could to secure seats
for the most popular shows of the time. He also ate at
good restaurants. The Savoy needs no explanation.
Hatchett's Restaurant was in Piccadilly, on the corner of
Albemarle Street, and was to become a celebrated jazz
venue in the Second World War. Scott's, a well-known
seafood restaurant, is still in existence in Mount Street.
The Grosvenor, where my grandfather spends his last night
of leave on 17 September, was the Grosvenor Hotel at
Victoria Station.

As for the other people with whom my grandfather socialised, they consisted predominantly of family and, in the case of Rita (Margarita Cameron Macdonald) and her relatives, family-to-be. My grandfather clearly got on very well with his father-in-law (John William Macdonald, or 'Grandpa Mac'), and was eventually appointed chief executor to his estate.

Rita, like McDougal in the diary, deserves a paragraph to herself. I remember her only as a nice old lady who talked to me in her kitchen. She was, however, by all accounts a strong and quietly supportive woman possessed of great insight, and reputedly even some psychic ability. Interestingly, in the light of my grandfather's assertion, in the case of McDougal, that he had 'rather a liking for those who are deaf', she was also substantially deaf, and had been so since being left too near an open window after contracting scarlet fever as a child. In spite of this, she became a fine pianist and accompanist, until sadly later in life she lost a little finger through intervening in a fight between two dogs. Her psychic ability apparently manifested itself mainly in great success in playing the stock market by intuition. It was her mother, Helen MacGregor Macdonald, however, from whom she inherited the trait, who had the experience most relevant to my grandfather's diary. The story goes that one day during the war she came into the house claiming that she had just seen and conversed with a relative (brother?) who was away at the front. He had told her that he had been killed, that he was perfectly fine and happy, and that she was not to worry; he had just come to say goodbye. Three days later, the telegram arrived.

On a less obviously supernatural note, Rita's insight into people proved invaluable years later, when my grandfather brought home a new and charming business partner. She warned my grandfather not to trust the man; rightly so, for he proceeded to try to sell the business behind my grandfather's back! In those days, business was conducted on a handshake and a shared system of values, and troublemakers were summarily dealt with. My grandfather had the man hounded out of the City.

The Faggs were the family of Alexander's mother, Alice. His father, William, and Col. Delavoye had each married one of the two 'beautiful Miss Faggs', renowned debutantes in their day and daughters of a Dr Fagg, a wealthy man who had a weakness for race meetings, and thereby lost all his money. Both the Faggs and the Bloxhams, the family from which his wife came, were apparently 'very old' English families. Hence the references to 'Lunch Faggs' and 'Call Faggs: see Duke'. It is not clear who or what 'Duke' was. He was no obvious relative; pure whimsy encourages me to fancy that he may have been the large dog (Marmaduke?) sitting with the good doctor in the portrait I still have of him.

The Princes were my grandfather's friend Guy Prince,

a wine importer, and his Swiss wife, Greta; according to my father, she made wonderful pancakes, and claimed, 'The only jam to have with pancakes is apricot!' Mrs Slocombe was evidently closely connected to the family, judging from the number of postcards I have both to and from her, but exactly what that connection was appears to have been forgotten. Maudie, as mentioned above, was the daughter of Col. Delavoye and Annie Fagg.

Lastly, one of the most interesting names of his dining companions is that of Nora, one of Rita's three German sisters-in-law, of whom the other two were Irma and Annie. Duncan Macdonald, Rita's brother (who served in the ASC and whom my grandfather sees occasionally in France), had known Annie Strauss from childhood days in the Wirral; their acquaintance continued in Germany, where they got engaged in 1906, before marrying in 1911. Duncan was educated in Heidelberg – a not uncommon practice for Englishmen prior to the war – and in the Macdonald family, as in others, there was much fraternisation between Germany and England. Thus it is not at all improbable that Nora should have been in England during the war – she had been born there and her sister was living there. The complication that might have affected dinner was that the women's brother, Walter, served in the Luftwaffe alongside the 'Red Baron', Von Richthofen, and was shot down and killed by the British. Presumably my grandfather did not mention his favourite 'sport' of watching aerial dogfights. Nora, incidentally, died only in 1989, one day before her 103rd birthday.[7]

As far as my grandfather's time spent outside London during the war is concerned, he takes a fishing holiday at Tomdoun prior to joining up, and makes two trips during his leave – one by car to Slapton with the Macdonalds in April 1917, and then, on his next leave, he spends ten days in Bognor, in early August.

The Tomdoun Sporting Lodge still exists, in Invergarry. It has been running since 1895, and continues to offer trout and pike fishing, stalking and shooting, alongside the opportunity for less bloodthirsty activities. It is reasonable to presume that the trip was to some extent organised with the specific intention of getting Tim's strength back up after his fever. One can imagine the delight with which the news of his leave extension was received. It is also interesting to note that Slapton by car from London in those days was a two-day journey. Google now tells me it should take about four hours.

Although not immediately relevant to my grandfather's experience, a point of note about Slapton Sands, near Kingsbridge, Devon, lies in the tragedy that was to befall it twenty-seven years later, in 1944, during Operation Tiger, a joint US and British exercise to prepare for D-Day. Some German E-boats happened upon the exercise, attacked, and chaos ensued, resulting in the deaths of over six hundred US servicemen, many due to 'friendly fire'; bodies continued to be washed up on the shore for weeks.

Bognor has thankfully not achieved such grisly distinction. It was bombed in the Second World War, but when my grandfather visited in 1917 it was still a rather genteel seaside resort, although developments had been occurring for a few years – the town already boasted three theatres, a cinema and a palatial entertainment centre called the 'Kursaal'.[8] My grandfather makes no reference to his leave in Bognor, other than to say that he spent it there. Whether or not he stayed there with Rita, no one knows. I rather hope he did.

The intention of this somewhat discursive foray into the details of my grandfather's social and family life has been to contribute, in a personal and intimate manner, to the picture of the man and the time he was living through. In many ways, it now seems such an alien world – entertainment was different, the role of women was different (intriguingly, though both brothers are mentioned, he never refers to any women in his family – sister Annie, mother, aunt?) and communication was much more difficult, both in the practical technological sense and in the sense that people exercised far more restraint in their personal interactions – there was not a lot of talk about one's 'feelings'.

And yet, for all that, we are really not so very different. The abiding impression I have of his leave is of what it must have felt like, for everyone, on that last day before he returned to the front: a constant stream of appointments – 'Guv', Uncle, Duke (even if he was a dog!), Maudie, Tommy, Jessica, the theatre, Rita seeing him off in the morning – all of them quietly desperate to see him before he left, all of them quietly conscious of the likelihood that he would never return, and all of them putting on the bravest faces they could muster, so as not to cause any upset. As his did, my heart sinks to think of it.

Captain Stewart in 1939.

NOTES

1 http://www.royalautomobileclub.co.uk/guestarea/rac.asp?s
   =ME&ss=HI.
2 John Earl and Michael Sell, *Guide to British Theatres 1750–1950*,
   Theatres Trust, 2000, pp. 109-10.
3 *Play Pictorial*, 24(147), 1914, quoted on
   http://library.kent.ac.uk/library/special/icons/playbills/play
   dat2.htm.
4 *Play Pictorial*, 29(175), 1916, quoted on
   http://library.kent.ac.uk/library/special/icons/playbills/play
   dat2.htm.
5 *Play Pictorial*, 29(174), 1916, quoted on
   http://library.kent.ac.uk/library/special/icons/playbills/play
   dat2.htm.
6 http://www.peopleplayuk.org.uk/guided_tours/musicals_tour/
   first_musicals/chu_chin_chow.php.
7 *The Alex and Ella Macdonald Memoirs*, compiled by Roddy
   Macdonald, Netherlands, 2007, p. 35.
8 http://www.localhistories.org/bognor.html.

ACKNOWLEDGEMENTS

BRINGING this to print has been an extraordinary journey. My thanks are due to everyone who helped, but especially to: Dr William Philpott and Jonathan Boff, Department of War Studies, King's College London; Tim and Jenny Barlass of Barlass e-Publishing; Robert Smith Literary Agency; Thomas Howard Stewart and Sally Stewart; Rupert Lancaster, Laura Macaulay and Kerry Hood at Hodder & Stoughton; Roddy Macdonald; Professor Richard Holmes; Jennifer Howard of TalkingIssues.com; Rowland Benbrook of Rbgraphics; Mark Lubbock of Ashurst. 'The General', and excerpts from *Memoirs of an Infantry Officer*, © Siegfried Sassoon are reproduced by kind permission of the Estate of George Sassoon. Excerpts from *Goodbye to All That*, © Robert Graves are reproduced by kind permission of Carcanet Press Limited.

PICTURE ACKNOWLEDGEMENTS

Getty Images: 35, 210, 220, 249, 252, 260. Imperial War Museum, London: 2, 7, 54, 81, 82, 108, 112, 138, 142, 145, 156, 157, 181, 190, 213, 235, 243. National Portrait Gallery, London: 114.

GLOSSARY

5.9	Heavy artillery gun (of 5.9-inch calibre)
9.2	Heavy artillery gun (of 9.2-inch calibre)
ADS	Advanced Dressing Station: the first stop for a wounded man
ASC	Army Service Corps: responsible for transport
Billet	Accommodation in a building
Bivouac	Accommodation in an open field
'B' Echelon	The transport and administration elements of a battalion left behind the lines when the unit went into battle. A number of fighting officers and men would also be left at 'B' Echelon to provide a cadre to reconstruct the battalion in the event of heavy losses in action

Boche	French nickname for Germans; used also by British
Box respirator	Gas mask
Brigade Scheme:	Brigade training exercise
CCS	Casualty Clearing Station: the second stop for a wounded man; from here he would be sent back to a hospital
CHQ	Company Headquarters
Communication trench	Trench running back from the front line to the support trenches and rear areas
CSM	Company Sergeant Major: the senior NCO in a company
Dugout	Underground shelter
Eighteen-pounder	Artillery gun
Estaminet	Small café serving simple food and, more importantly, wine and beer
Extended order	Tactical formation, where men kept seven to nine paces apart
Fire step	Step built into a trench on which sentries and defenders could stand to raise their heads above the parapet, enabling them to see and fire
Flea bag	Slang for sleeping bag
GOC	General Officer Commanding
HE	High explosive
HLI	Highland Light Infantry

Howitzer	Artillery piece
Loophole	Hole left in a steel plate, built into the parapet, to enable observation or fire
MG	Machine gun
Mills bomb	Egg-shaped hand grenade, as used by the British army until well after the Second World War
Mine	Both sides tried to dig tunnels under the enemy positions, pack them with explosive and detonate them, blowing up the defenders and their trench
Mustard gas	Chemical weapon which blisters the skin and causes blindness
NCO	Non-Commissioned Officer, e.g. sergeant
OC	Officer Commanding
Officer's servant	Officers were permitted a personal servant, drawn from the ranks. Later known as a 'batman'
OTC	Officer Training Corps: cadet units at schools and universities
Parados	Earth or sandbags piled behind a trench to protect occupants from a blast from the rear
Parapet	Earth or sandbags piled in front of a trench to protect occupants from bullets, etc., from the front

RAMC	Royal Army Medical Corps
RE	Royal Engineers
RFC	Royal Flying Corps. Became Royal Air Force in 1918
Rum ration	A quarter-gill tot of rum (equivalent to a generous double today), distributed to soldiers daily at dawn, when the Medical Officer considered, and the Divisional Commander agreed, that conditions were tough. Most divisions deemed conditions tough every day. The 33rd Division was a notorious exception.
RWF	Royal Welch Fusiliers
SR	Scottish Rifles. Alternative name for Stewart's regiment. (Note: a further alternative 'nickname', not generally used to a soldier's face, was 'The Poison Dwarfs' [sic], an account of the preponderance of 'wee Glaswegian hard men' in its ranks.)
Stokes gun	Mortar
Strafe	Artillery bombardment; also any argument
Town Major	Officer in charge of finding billets for troops arriving in a town
TT	Teetotaller

Very light	Flare, fired from a handgun
Wiz bang	Kind of German artillery shell
Wiring party	Group of men sent into no man's land to erect or repair barbed-wire defences
Zero time	The planned hour of an attack

BIBLIOGRAPHY

Ashworth, Tony, *Trench Warfare 1914–1918: The Live and Let Live System* (London and Basingstoke: Macmillan, 1980)

Audoin-Rouzeau, Stephane and Becker, Annette, *1914–1918: Understanding the Great War* (trans. Catherine Temerson) (London: Profile, 2002)

Bacon, Alban F. L., *The Wanderings of a Temporary Warrior: A Territorial Officer's Narrative of Service (and Sport) in three Continents* (London: H. F. & G. Witherby, 1922)

Beckett, Ian F. W., *The Great War 1914–1918* (Harlow: Pearson Education, 2001)

Bickersteth, John (ed.), *The Bickersteth Diaries 1914–1918* (London: Leo Cooper, 1995)

Blunden, Edmund, *Undertones of War* (London: Collins, 1965; first published 1928)

Bond, Brian (ed.), *The First World War and British Military History* (Oxford: Clarendon Press, 1991)

Bond, Brian, *The Unquiet Western Front: Britain's Role in*

Literature and History (Cambridge: Cambridge University Press, 2002)

Bourke, Joanna, *An Intimate History of Killing: Face-to-Face Killing in Twentieth Century Warfare* (London: Granta, 2000)

British Commission for Military History, *'Look to Your Front!': Studies in the First World War* (Staplehurst: Spellmount, 1999)

Brown, Malcolm, *The Imperial War Museum Book of the Somme* (London: Sidgwick & Jackson, 1996)

Cecil, Hugh and Liddle, Peter, (eds), *Facing Armageddon: The First World War Experienced* (London: Leo Cooper, 1996)

Chapman, Guy, *A Passionate Prodigality: Fragments of Autobiography* (London: Ivor Nicholson & Watson, 1933)

Chapman, Guy, (ed.), *Vain Glory: A Miscellany of the Great War 1914–1918 written by those who fought in it on each side and on all fronts* (London: Cassell, 1937)

Cloete, Stuart, *A Victorian Son: An Autobiography 1897–1922* (London: Collins, 1972)

Corrigan, Gordon, *Mud, Blood and Poppycock: Britain and the First World War* (London: Cassell, 2003)

Dunn, J. C., *The War the Infantry Knew* (London: Jane's, 1987; first published 1938)

Edmonds, James, *History of the Great War Based on Official Documents: Military Operations France and Belgium 1917*, vol. II: *Messines and Third Ypres (Passchendaele)* (London: HMSO, 1948)

Eksteins, Modris, *Rites of Spring: The Great War and the Birth of the Modern Age* (London: Bantam, 1989)

Ellis, John, *Eye-Deep in Hell* (London: Penguin, 2002)

Falls, Cyril, *History of the Great War Based on Official Documents: Military Operations France and Belgium 1917,* vol. I: *The German Retreat to the Hindenburg Line and the Battles of Arras* (London: Macmillan, 1940)

Ferguson, Niall, *The Pity of War* (London: Allen Lane, 1998)

Fraser, David (ed.), *In Good Company: The First World War Letters and Diaries of the Hon. William Fraser, Gordon Highlanders* (Salisbury: Michael Russell, 1990)

Fussell, Paul, *The Great War and Modern Memory* (New York: Oxford University Press, 1975)

Gilbert, Martin, *Somme: The Heroism and Horror of War* (London: John Murray, 2006)

Graham, Stephen, *A Private in the Guards* (London: Macmillan, 1919)

Graves, Robert, *Goodbye to All That* (London: Penguin, 2000; first published 1929)

Gray, J. Glenn, *The Warriors: Reflections on Men in Battle* (New York: Harper & Row, 1967)

Hart, Peter, *The Somme* (London: Weidenfeld & Nicolson, 2003)

Holmes, Richard, *Acts of War: The Behaviour of Men in Battle* (London: Weidenfeld & Nicolson, 2003)

Holmes, Richard, *Tommy: The British Soldier on the Western Front, 1914–1918* (London: HarperCollins, 2004)

Howard, Michael, *The First World War* (Oxford: Oxford University Press, 2002)

Hynes, Samuel, *A War Imagined: The First World War and English Culture* (London: Bodley Head, 1990)

Jackson, John, *Private 12768: Memoir of a Tommy* (Stroud: Tempus, 2005)

Kelly, D. V., *39 Months: With the 'Tigers', 1915–1918* (London: Ernest Benn, 1930)

Klein, Holger (ed.), *The First World War in Fiction: A Collection of Critical Essays* (London: Macmillan, 1976)

Leed, Eric J., *No Man's Land: Combat and Identity in World War I* (Cambridge: Cambridge University Press, 1979)

Liddle, Peter, Bourne, John and Whitehead, Ian (eds), *The Great World War 1914–1945*, vol. I: *Lightning Strikes Twice* (London: HarperCollins, 2000)

Lyttelton, Oliver (Viscount Chandos), *From Peace to War: A Study in Contrast 1857–1918* (London: Bodley Head, 1968)

Macdonald, Lyn, *They Called It Passchendaele* (London: Michael Joseph, 1978)

Macdonald, Lyn, *Somme* (London: Michael Joseph, 1983)

Manning, Frederic, *Her Privates We* (London: Serpent's Tail, 1999)

Masefield, John, *Great War: Collected Works* (ed. Philip W. Errington) (Barnsley: Pen & Sword Military, 2007)

Messenger, Charles, *Call to Arms: The British Army 1914–18* (London: Weidenfeld & Nicolson, 2005)

Miles, Wilfrid, *History of the Great War Based on Official Documents: Military Operations France and Belgium 1916*, vol. II: *2nd July 1916 to the End of the Battles of the Somme* (London: Macmillan, 1938)

Montague, C. E., *Disenchantment* (London: Chatto & Windus, 1922)

Moran, Lord, *The Anatomy of Courage* (London: Constable, 1966; first published 1945)

Nicholls, Jonathan, *Cheerful Sacrifice: The Battle of Arras 1917* (London: Leo Cooper, 1993)

Norman, Terry, *The Hell They Called High Wood: The Somme 1916* (Wellingborough: Patrick Stephens, 1989; first published 1984)

Prior, Robin and Wilson, Trevor, *Command on the Western Front: The Military Career of Sir Henry Rawlinson 1914–1918* (Oxford: Blackwell, 1992)

Prior, Robin and Wilson, Trevor, *Passchendaele: The Untold Story* (New Haven and London: Yale University Press, 1996)

Prior, Robin and Wilson, Trevor, *The Somme* (New Haven and London: Yale University Press, 2005)

Richards, Frank, *Old Soldiers Never Die* (Peterborough: Krijnen and Langley, 2004; first published 1933)

Sassoon, Siegfried, *Memoirs of an Infantry Officer* (London: Faber, 1965; first published 1930)

Sheffield, G. D., *Leadership in the Trenches: Officer–Man Relations, Morale and Discipline in the British Army in the*

Era of the First World War (Basingstoke & London: Macmillan, 2000)

Sheffield, Gary, *Forgotten Victory: The First World War: Myths and Realities* (London: Headline Review, 2002)

Story, H. H., *History of the Cameronians (Scottish Rifles)*, vol. II: *1910–1933* (privately published, 1961)

Strachan, Hew, *The First World War*, vol. I: *To Arms* (Oxford: Oxford University Press, 2001)

Strachan, Hew, *The First World War: A New Illustrated History* (London: Simon and Schuster, 2003)

Todman, Dan, *The Great War: Myth and Memory* (London: Hambledon and London, 2005)

Travers, Tim, *The Killing Ground: The British Army, the Western Front and the Emergence of Modern War 1900–1918* (Barnsley: Pen & Sword, 2003)

Westlake, Ray, *British Battalions on the Somme 1916* (Barnsley: Leo Cooper, 1994)

Wilson, Trevor, *The Myriad Faces of War: Britain and the Great War, 1914–1918* (Cambridge: Polity, 1986)

Winter, Denis, *Death's Men: Soldiers of the Great War* (London: Allen Lane, 1978)

INDEX

Figures in italics indicate illustrations.